NON-MANIPULATIVE SELLING

NON-MANIPULATIVE
SELLING

Anthony J. Alessandra, Ph.D.
Alessandra & Associates, Inc.
La Jolla, California

and Phillip S. Wexler
Phillip S. Wexler & Associates
Atlanta, Georgia

with Jerry D. Deen
PSH Business Systems
Honolulu, Hawaii

Reston Publishing Company, Inc.
A Prentice-Hall Company
Reston, Virginia

LIBRARY OF CONGRESS CATALOGING IN PUBLICATION DATA

Alessandra, Anthony J.
  Non-manipulative selling.

   1. Selling. I. Wexler, Phillip S. II. Deen,
Jerry D. III. Title
HF5438.25.A43 1981   658.8'5   81-4973
ISBN 0-8359-4936-2   AACR2
ISBN 0-8359-4935-4 (pbk.)

Manuscript Editor — Renata V. Schmidt

Book Design & Illustrations — Tracy C. Sabin

10 9 8 7 6 5 4 3

Printed in the United States of America

For Janice
for her patience, understanding, and help
during the long writing process

Contents

Preface

Selling provides, perhaps, the most challenging, interesting, diversified, and rewarding of all careers. Selling is not just a job, but a profession which requires a vast knowledge of products, services, and human behavior. A good salesperson is a true professional.

You will find this book responsive to the needs of the professional salesperson. You may also find the book to be a "radical" departure from academic and traditional sales texts. It views selling as a problem-solving process rather than a persuasion process. It regards the salesperson as a professional business counselor rather than a "pusher" of products. It holds the consumer as king and not just a pawn in the game of selling. It espouses a situational and individualistic approach to the sales process as opposed to a canned approach.

Non-Manipulative Selling will undoubtedly rattle the cages of traditional salespeople who rely predominantly on their speaking skills, objection-handling skills, and closing techniques to make the sale. It is meant to do that.

Non-Manipulative Selling will disturb traditional sales managers and sales trainers who rely predominantly on the hard sell. They may shun non-manipulative selling, thinking of it as a soft sell approach. If "soft sell" means that you run from the customer at the first sign of resistance, they are wrong. If "soft sell" means that you do not ask for the order, they are wrong. If "soft sell" means that you treat the customer with respect, communicate openly, and avoid sales when they are truly not in the best interest of the customer, they are right. Fortunately, for us, non-manipulative selling works better than the hard sell. Not only does it lead to more sales, but it makes people feel better about dealing with you and allows you to feel better about yourself and your occupation. That is the bottom-line benefit of non-manipulative selling.

This book has evolved out of several years of refinement through seminars and on-the-line work with people who live by selling and who want to live better by selling better. Many people helped make this book a reality. I wish to express my sincere thanks to all of them.

Foremost appreciation goes to Phillip S. Wexler and Jerry D. Deen. The whole concept of Non-Manipulative Selling started in Atlanta, Georgia with Phillip S. Wexler while I was teaching marketing at Georgia State University. Phil and I began a sales and management training and consulting company to market Non-Manipulative Selling seminars. Together we conceptualized the program and wrote the initial version of it, refining it over a period of more than two years. Without Phil, *Non-Manipulative Selling* might not have come into existence. The finished product came to fruition with additional conceptual and writing help from Jerry D. Deen. Jerry also motivated me to finish writing the book now rather than some time in the future.

Special thanks goes to Renata V. Schmidt. She provided invaluable input in the form of restructuring and editing the material to make it easier to read, learn, and teach. The quality of the book was enhanced considerably through her assistance.

Gratitude also goes to the thousands of salespeople and sales managers who attended the Non-Manipulative Selling seminars since 1976. Their input and comments helped shape the material into a practical success-oriented book.

Finally, I wish to thank all of the sales, management, and communications experts who directly or indirectly contributed the concepts that serve as the backbone of *Non-Manipulative Selling*. The work of Carl Rogers in humanistic psychology, William Glasser in reality therapy, and Jack Gibb in trust and openness permeates this entire book. The work of Carl Jung, Albert Mehrabian, David W. Merrill, and others contributed greatly to the behavioral styles sections. Gerald W. Faust provided significant input in the communications section. R.G. Nichols, Carl Rogers, and others indirectly contributed to the listening and feedback sections. The research of John T. Molloy, Leonard Zunin, Chris L. Kleinke, and others helped shape the image section. Writings by Edward T. Hall, Julius Fast, and Gerard Nierenberg, and others helped shape the body language and proxemics sections. Others, such as Tom Alexander, Bill Arens, Bill Cantrell, Rod Hansen, Mike Hoerr, Charles Holt, Phillip Hunsaker, Phil Lee, Ralph Longfellow, Virginia Manasse, David J. Schwartz, Bill Schwarz, Brian Sellstrom, Gary Sheets, Carol Dresen Stonehocker, Dave Stork, Paul Vadnais, and Pete Wheeler, provided important input, mental stimulation, motivation, and encouragement. My meager thanks cannot begin to repay their unselfish contributions that helped mold *Non-Manipulative Selling* as it exists today. Without them, I would have had to reinvent the wheel instead of redesigning it.

AJA

List of Figures

Foreword

I was delighted when Tony Alessandra asked me to read the final draft of his book, *Non-Manipulative Selling*. I like it very much. I feel it will encourage many talented people to pursue selling as a career. *Non-Manipulative Selling* forsakes selling as a battle and becomes a people-centered, problem-solving activity that can be exciting and rewarding.

Tony and I have known each other for more than a decade. He has always exhibited unusual professionalism. From the beginning of our relationship, I noted that Dr. Alessandra does not subscribe to the idea that you must intimidate a person to make a sale. Not only are these approaches questionable, but *they do not work except once or twice.* Invariably, most of us can be fooled, but only a very few of us can be deceived by the same person several times. And in selling, repeat business makes you the real money.

Non-Manipulative Selling puts the salesperson in the role of a professional consultant, a problem solver who specializes in diagnosing the prospect's needs and then satisfying them. The salesperson and the prospect sit on the same side of the desk, so to speak. They are two important people meeting to discuss something of mutual importance.

I think you will profit from *Non-Manipulative Selling*. It teaches what salespeople need to know and practice to maximize their success. For example, Chapter 5 on "Listening" is excellent for it explains clearly the WHY and HOW of paying attention to what prospects say. Chapter 7 tells us how to design a personal self-image — how to better "package" ourselves for successful selling. Chapter 8 contains excellent ideas on how to use body language to get desired results.

Part II of *Non-Manipulative Selling* stresses the steps to follow to make things happen. They are simple and practical but so often overlooked.

Many of the ideas presented in *Non-Manipulative Selling* have long been practiced by the small minority of salespeople who are already highly successful. But Tony Alessandra is the first to put these concepts together in a cohesive, easy-to-understand form.

After I reviewed his manuscript, I told Tony, "It's great. I know it will help a lot of people earn more money and enjoy greater peace of mind." Regardless of whether you are a highly successful professional salesperson, just beginning, or just thinking about getting into sales, Non-Manipulative Selling can help you.

I also recommend this book to professional managers. After all, the key to successful managing is selling people ideas.

Non-Manipulative Selling is a contribution to the literature. It will help you earn more. And very importantly, it will help you enjoy selling.

David J. Schwartz
Author of *The Magic of Thinking Big*

Dr. Anthony J. Alessandra, a member of the National Speakers Association, is a professional speaker and trainer averaging 100 speeches per year for thousands of people at national seminars, workshops, conventions, sales rallies and spouses' programs. His speeches and seminars cover the subjects of professional selling skills, the art of managing people, the power of effective listening, communicating effectively, and balancing your personal and professional lives.

Tony is also a respected co-author of *The Art of Managing People* and is a contributing author of two additional books, *Build a Better You — Starting Now!*, Vol. II, and *The Competitive Edge in Selling*. His syndicated articles appear in many magazines across the country on a monthly basis.

Tony was featured in the award-winning CRM/McGraw-Hill film "The Power of Listening." He is also the co-author of the multi-media training module "Listening to Communicate" published by the McGraw-Hill Book Company.

Walt Disney Training and Development Company, a division of Walt Disney Productions, has signed a long-term contract with Tony to produce a series of sales training films that Walt Disney Productions plans to market to business and industry throughout the world.

A former sales manager and award-winning salesman in direct consumer sales, Tony taught sales and marketing courses at the university level for eight and one-half years.

A native of New York City, Tony now resides in La Jolla, California with his wife Janice and their son Justin.

You may contact Tony by writing or calling:

ALLESSANDRA AND ASSOCIATES, INC.
PO Box 2767
La Jolla, CA 92038
(714) 459-1515

Phillip S. Wexler, also a member of the National Speakers Association, in addition to speaking and training at approximately thirty conventions, rallies, seminars and workshops, has custom designed and conducted training programs for a number of companies throughout the United States.

Phil's programs are designed to educate and entertain. His speeches and seminars cover the subjects and professional selling, the art of managing people, effective listening, and effective communications both in the business world and in everyday life. Having gained national recognition in the area of Sales and Management, Phil is recognized as one of the nation's leading authorities on projecting a professional image.

Phil is a respected author, contributing to *The Art of Managing People* and *Building A Better You Starting Now!*. His articles have appeared in newspapers and magazines nationwide.

Phil has made guest appearances on a variety of radio and television shows. His audio cassettes are considered a must for every sales office library.

A former Vice President of Marketing and award winning salesman, Phil's practical marketing experience in consumer sales affords him tremendous credibility with the salespeople with whom he works daily. "He's been there, and knows what it's like."

A native of New Jersey, Phil now resides with his wife Sue and daughter Ashley in Atlanta, Georgia.

For additional information, write or call:

PHILLIP S. WEXLER & ASSOCIATES
Post Office Box 19872
Atlanta, Georgia 30325-0872
(404) 993-5700

Jerry D. Deen is a specialist in recognizing and solving internal problems related to profit. His expertise in competitive marketing methods and organizational communication enable him to serve clients such as Union Bank, Western States Advertising Association, National Softwood Sales, WTC Airfreight, and National Business Systems.

Mr. Deen received a B.S. in Marketing Management and Research and an M.B.A. in Marketing from California State University at Los Angeles.

In addition to consulting and training assignments with local and national firms, Mr. Deen has held instructional positions in Marketing, Management and Salesmanship with several colleges and universities including the University of Redlands, LaVerne University, Rio Hondo College, and California State University at Fullerton.

Mr. Deen is president of PSH Business Systems in Honolulu, Hawaii.

Learn While You Drive With
NON-MANIPULATIVE SELLING
CASSETTE TAPES

Learn from professionally produced audio cassette tapes while driving to work and waiting for appointments, or review these tapes as often as you wish during leisure time at home. Accompanying booklet contains illustrations to augment the material presented in the tapes — it's the same seminar Dr. Alessandra teaches nationwide for $440.

There are sixteen easy-to-listen-to and easy-to-put-into-practice sections that will give you numerous practical ideas that you can put to work immediately.

The tapes are not a verbal transcription of the book. They include clear, easy-to-understand explanations for many of the concepts in this book, plus new information learned best by listening. A must for motivated people who make every second count.

Included are eight cassettes with booklet (nearly 7 hours of material), packaged bookstyle in hard vinyl for protection while traveling. Retail price $95.00/set (includes shipping; California residents add $5.70 sales tax). If paying by credit card, give us name (Mastercard or Visa), credit card number, and expiration date. All orders carry a 30-day Unconditional Money-Back Guarantee.

Send your orders to:

ALLESSANDRA AND ASSOCIATES, INC.
PO Box 2767
La Jolla, CA 92038
(714) 459-1515

PHILLIP S. WEXLER & ASSOCIATES
Post Office Box 19872
Atlanta, Georgia 30325-0872
(404) 993-5700

NOW AVAILABLE!

FILMS AND VIDEOTAPES BASED ON *NON-MANIPULATIVE SELLING*

© MCMLXXX Walt Disney Productions
Printed in USA

...From **Walt Disney Productions**

Produced with the assistance of Anthony J. Alessandra, Ph.D., co-author of *Non-Manipulative Selling*, these hard-hitting films will help you take the commonsense lessons of this book and apply them to everyday sales situations.

Now salespeople, sales managers, and CEO's can see for themselves the exciting opportunities presented by Non-Manipulative Selling-in films created with that special Disney magic for today's professional salesperson.

To learn how your company can acquire these exciting new training materials, contact: Walt Disney Training and Development Programs, 500 South Buena Vista Street, Dept. A, Burbank, California 91521. (213) 840-1707.

1

Removing Pressure and Still Getting the Sale

IMAGINE WHAT would happen to our society if every salesperson went on strike today. All of them. Some businesses would close almost immediately. Others would hang on while "management" tried to fill the sales role. Ultimately, the effects of closures and inefficiencies would be so widespread that every business would experience drastic results.

To see this, picture the world of business as a complex pipeline system. The salesperson is at the end of that system controlling the business flow valve. What every salesperson does has an effect which is felt through many systems. For example, if an automobile salesperson does not sell, the dealership suffers. Management and administrative staff may need to be curtailed. If dealerships sell less, they order less and factory business slows — again, employment drops. If the automotive factories slow down, so must the production of parts and raw materials, including radios, mirrors, plastics, sheet metal, and steel. Finally, the effects are felt by those who mine or grow the natural resources such as iron, copper, and cotton.

Of course, one salesperson can be replaced if he is not performing. But look at the effect, the power. As with the automobile industry, individual salespeople in *any* business can affect the economy of the entire business and, in a real way, the economy of the nation.

Then, too, selling is a professional area of expertise that goes beyond the sale of products. Ideas, treaties, candidates, and a variety of services must also be "sold." From the local merchant to heads of state negotiating treaties, selling directly affects all of our lives. It has been said, and it certainly is true, that "Nothing happens until someone sells something" — nothing good, that is.

Salespeople are among the highest paid professionals in our society. They are obviously important to our economy. Why, then, do so few people respect sales as a career? Employee turnover is higher in sales positions than in almost any other occupation. Ask college students if they want to be salespeople and you get a resounding "NO!" And yet, a large number of them will be in a sales position shortly after graduation. To save face, they call themselves "sales engineers," "sales consultants," "marketing representatives," "account representatives," and so forth. But a rose by any other name...

Why the lack of popularity? Why is one of our oldest and most important business professions looked down upon by the public as well as the practitioners themselves? The answer, in one word, is — PRESSURE! Internal, tension-inducing pressure causes the salesperson and every client he contacts to feel uneasy, displeased, and distrustful of the interaction.

Traditional sales continues to focus on domination and control by the seller over the buyer. The salesperson is taught techniques by the hundreds: techniques to ask questions that always result in "Yes" answers, techniques to handle any objection, "closing" techniques designed to maneuver even the most reluctant buyer into the position where he almost has to say "Yes" ("Uncle!").

2

The name "closing" itself discloses the one-sided manipulative philosophy. The old way — "Create Need," "Fill Need," "Close! Close! Close!" — forces the salesperson to "close in" on the buyer. If the prospect says, "No"·

Roll up your sleeves.

Overcome those objections.

And close!

Close!

Close!

Is it any wonder that salespeople sometime feel bad about themselves and their profession? When you spend your days persuading people in a manner which can be construed as exploitative and manipulative, you can't help but feel bad about yourself. And when you cannot persuade the client to say "Yes," even though the client may really have no need of the services, you are taught to analyze why you failed to close. Failed!

The nature of today's buyers adds still more to this pressure on the traditional salesperson. They are better educated, have greater exposure to media information, and have developed a strong aversion to exploitation and manipulation. They have lost tolerance for the domineering salesperson who seeks to control them. You know or can imagine the tensions that arise as the salesperson — who also hates to be manipulated — tries to control buyers with standard dominating sales techniques.

Such pressure is NOT a natural function of selling. It does not have to go with the job. It shouldn't and it doesn't have to be this way! This is what non-manipulative selling is all about:

How to avoid tension-inducing pressure.

How to stop attempting to manipulate people.

How to build a relationship of mutual trust.

and

How to increase your sales while enjoying it more.

Non-manipulative selling overcomes the unhealthy, tension-laden sales environment. It is not a new bag of tricks. There are no surefire gimmicks. In fact, it is a fresh look at some very long-standing and respected techniques used in clinical psychology, counseling, consulting, negotiating, management, and marketing. These nonexploitative techniques have been adapted to the selling environment according to the philosophy that it is neither healthy nor productive in the long run to attempt to manipulate and control other people. In fact, an overriding claim of non-manipulative selling is that:

People buy services or products most often because they feel that they and their problems are understood by the seller — not because the buyer is made to understand the product by an insistent salesperson.

Four guiding principles support this. Note how they reflect a client-centered approach.

Governing Principles of Non-Manipulative Selling

1. The sales process should be built around trust bond relationships that require openness and honesty on the part of both client and salesperson.

2. Clients buy because the salesperson truly understands and appreciates their business-related problems, not solely because the client understands the salesperson's product or service.

3. People strive for the right to make their own decisions, even if they are poor decisions. They resent being manipulated, controlled, or persuaded, even if the solution is valid.

4. If you impose solutions upon clients, they will resent both you and your solution. Pinpoint problems, but don't solve them; let the client solve them with your consultative help.

Not following these principles can result in a loss of sales, prestige, or both. An example of a young salesperson comes to mind. After attending a motivational, go-get-em-tiger sales meeting, he called on a new account with the attitude not to take "No" for an answer. After a long discussion and many closing attempts, he finally got a $150 initial order. He also received the results of a phone call that the customer placed to his firm. She liked the firm's products, but demanded that they never again send that salesperson to see her. It cost her $150 to get rid of the salesperson and reduce her tension. It cost the salesperson the account and the loss of prestige associated with customer complaints concerning inappropriate personal behavior — a poor trade-off by most standards.

Non-manipulative selling allows the buyer to feel that he has "bought" — not that he has been "sold." The client operates from a heightened position of openness and trust because the seller avoids exploitation. Instead of "He'll tell you what you want to hear to get a sale," the salesperson using these guidelines is known for telling them "how it is" — even if it means no sale today. In the long run, and surprisingly in the short run, sales will increase; clients will be more loyal; and, if you're the trust-building salesperson, you'll feel better about yourself and your occupation.

A well-known but startling example of the impact of non-manipulation is the experience of Fred Clarkson, who bet he could sell more $5 bills for $10 than a traditional salesperson could sell $10 bills for $5. The contest took place that evening in downtown Boston. Each man was allowed to make 20 attempts, and the one who had the most sales was the winner. Fred won, six sales to two. In asking the six (who had obviously made poor purchases) why they had agreed to buy a $5 bill for $10, all six stated that they knew it was a poor trade but that they bought because something inside them told them it was the right thing to do. In asking the 18 who refused to pay $5 for a $10 bill, all stated that they knew it was an excellent trade but they opposed the manipulative techniques of the salesperson.[1]

So non-manipulative selling is different from traditional sales. It requires a different way of thinking about the customer, the product, and the goals of the sales process. The two lists which follow

---

1. Excerpted from *The Entrepreneur's Manual,* by Richard M. White, Jr., Copyright 1977 by the author. Reprinted with the permission of the publisher, Chilton Book Company, Radnor, Pennsylvania.

point out clearly some of the major differences. They are characteristics which result from careful application of their respective selling techniques. Do you recognize anyone in either list?

Traditional Selling	Non-Manipulative Selling
Salesperson oriented	Client oriented
Creates needs	Discovers needs
"Talks at" client	"Discusses with" client
Makes sales	Makes customers
Inflexible	Adaptable
Increases fear and distrust	Increases trust and understanding

The list makes several obvious points. Traditional selling is salesperson oriented. The actions of the salesperson are directed toward fulfilling personal needs by the shortest, most direct route. The traditional salesperson "persuades" the customer to see his or her point of view — to MAKE THE SALE the overriding goal. In non-manipulative selling, however, your goal is to MAKE A CUSTOMER. Note that we said a "customer," not necessarily a friend, but rather a person who respects your opinion, trusts your recommendations, and buys from you on a repeat basis because of that trust and respect for your professional approach. A sale today is nice, and it is usually profitable. However, the real payoff to a salesperson comes from follow-up orders placed without the necessity of persistent time-consuming sales calls.

Applying the principles of non-manipulative selling results in reduced levels of fear, distrust, and interpersonal tension that can create severe problems for salespeople. High levels of fear and distrust result in defensiveness, communication barriers, and non-productive and counterproductive games. When this situation occurs, tensions increase in both the salesperson and the client and the "objection game" begins. Gone is the attitude of true problem solving. Instead, the situation becomes one of persuasion, exploitation, and control. The client defensively thinks up as many objections as possible, justified or not, to prevent the salesperson from breaking through his defenses. The salesperson resorts to more techniques to counteract the objections. It is an interesting game for a cocktail party, but it certainly is not a way to make a career rewarding — monetarily or psychologically. In the objection game there are no winners — only losers.

But how do you actually SELL in this non-manipulative way? First, you need to practice and then apply a new set of processes, shown in Table 1 at the end of this chapter. These are fairly easy to state, but like every new skill, they take real desire and practice to use in an easy, effective way. Second, you need to acquire very special tension-reducing communication skills. Every step — the whole process — is built upon a trust bond that either exists or is lacking between the salesperson and the client. When two or more people get together, a natural tension can exist. If it's a sales situation, the interpersonal tension generally increases. Depending on how the people relate to each other, the tension can either increase or decrease. Have you ever met someone that you felt you knew all of your life after only ten minutes, and another person with whom you could never get comfortable? — high interpersonal tension.

If interpersonal tension increases or remains high, the trust bond between those people weakens. As the trust bond weakens, credibility decreases and so does the probability of a sale — no matter what you are "selling." If, however, you can decrease the tension level, the opposite is true — trust increases, credibility increases, and the probability of a sale increases.

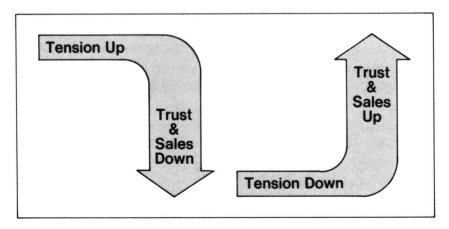

It is a simple equation, and yet it remains a problem. Why? One of the major reasons, if not THE major reason, for increasing tension levels is the failure of people to behave or communicate appropriately with their clients. There is some truth to the old saying, "It isn't what you ask — it's how you ask it." Most salespeople do not deliberately behave in a manner that increases tension. They may not realize that their actions are increasing tension, and even when they sense heightening tension, they may not know how to act appropriately. It is interesting to note that some of the older "traditional" sales training programs that many of us have experienced were designed so that, if you were any good with them, you created high tension levels by doing something "right." Are you still using those tension-producing communication techniques?

A major portion of this book centers on helping you learn ways to build the trust bond. It explores those tension-reducing communication techniques so crucial to applying the non-manipulative selling process effectively. The other portion of this book outlines the non-manipulative selling processes and goes on to detail ways to carry them out. If you achieve the skill steps mentioned, you will be able to sell without pressure; you will tend to increase your sales and, at the same time, enjoy your profession. Quite a powerful payoff, isn't it?

Table 1

THE NON-MANIPULATIVE SELLING PROCESS*

1. **DEFINE THE NEED(S)/PROBLEM(S)**

   a. Establish the trust bond.
   b. Determine the current situation.
   c. Determine client goals and objectives.
   d. Identify client needs and problems.
   e. Agree on the needs and problems to be worked on.

2. **FIND A SOLUTION**

   a. Check the trust bond.
   b. Determine decision-making criteria.
   c. Solicit potential solutions.
   d. Suggest potential solutions.
   e. Agree upon the best solution(s).

3. **IMPLEMENT THE SOLUTION**

   a. Check the trust bond.
   b. Outline each other's tasks and responsibilities.
   c. Work out an implementation schedule.

4. **TRACK THE RESULTS**

   a. Check the trust bond.
   b. Identify criteria for successful results.
   c. Determine how and when to measure results.
   d. Monitor the results.

* All steps are to be done mutually with the client.

Part I
Building Trust

Some salespeople seem to be able to create trust without trying. Clients seek their opinions and enjoy their company. Lucky? Well, perhaps; but most of them apply techniques which almost anyone can learn, given good guidance and direction. These techniques center on three basic skills:

1. *Identification of client behavioral style.*

2. *Recognition and use of communication techniques.*

3. *Application of behavioral flexibility: Using communication techniques that work with client styles.*

They are the key to creating that trust bond so necessary to non-manipulative selling. Part I is organized to forward these skills.

Chapters associated with Part I are:

2

How To "Size Up" Prospects

UPON MEETING someone, you invariably form distinct first impressions of that person. Of course, others do the same of you. Regardless of whether or not these impressions are accurate, you tend to treat each other as if they were and react accordingly. If your impressions are correct, your relationship with the other person more than likely will start on the right foot, and the trust bond can start to develop. However, if you misjudge the other person, your subsequent behavior may be inappropriate with that person and tensions and distrust may build.

A crucial skill in building trust, then, is the ability to form accurate impressions. This requires interpreting a client's "behavioral style," noting those actions which indicate how the client wants to be treated. The non-manipulative approach depends upon it.

To begin to justify behavioral style is fairly simple; being good at it takes work. This chapter is designed to help. First, it presents the concept of behavioral styles and points out specific style characteristics. Then it presents ways to rapidly identify the specific behavioral styles of clients. This provides a powerful tool which, when used with the communication techniques of Chapter 3, will allow you to treat people the way they indicate they want to be treated. The net result is decreased tension and increased trust: a better selling environment.

Behavioral Style Characteristics

People act and react to others in many ways. Identification of behavioral style centers on the "observable aspects" of people's behavior — those physical, verbal, or nonverbal actions that people display when others are present. When people consistently reflect actions which indicate a specific behavioral style, they also tend to be described by common sets of characteristics. This section of the chapter uses these characteristics to help you understand the concept of behavioral styles. Then you will be prepared to observe real actions and categorize real people.

Undirected, you could observe and try to catalog thousands of behaviors in any one person. That would quickly become an exercise in futility. But, identifying behavioral style is possible. You begin by classifying a client's behavior on two dimensions:

RESPONSIVENESS

and

ASSERTIVENESS

It is much like measuring a foot for a shoe — make it wide enough for the widest part and long enough for the longest part, and the rest of the foot will fit someplace in between.

The following definitions are kept simple in order to make them easier to remember and use:

RESPONSIVENESS: The readiness with which a person both outwardly shows emotions or feelings and develops relationships.

ASSERTIVENESS: The amount of control and forcefulness a person attempts to exercise over other people, their thoughts, and their emotions — or over situations.

Responsiveness and assertiveness levels vary across individuals, and any one person may be high in one and low in the other — or somewhere between. In other words, we all have some level of responsiveness and some level of assertiveness.

*The style model referred to herein is the authors' adaptation of original research and data compiled since 1964 by David W. Merrill, Ph.D. For a comprehensive understanding of Dr. Merrill's work, see: *Personal Styles* and *Effective Performance*, Merrill and Reid, Chilton 1981 or write The TRACOM Corp., 200 Fillmore Street, Denver, Colo. 80206.

For instance, I recall a client with whom I eventually had a highly successful sales relationship. My first appointment was made by her secretary for 10:10 a.m. (not 10:00 or 10:30). As I arrived a few minutes early, the secretary had me sit in the reception area. My future client came out of her office, acknowledged my presence with a polite "canned" smile, and gave a list of detailed instructions to the secretary. I noticed she was meticulously dressed. Then, with another polite smile, she asked me to follow her into the office, told me where to sit, looked at her watch, phoned her secretary to hold all calls for fifteen minutes, hung up, looked at her watch again, and said, "You have 15 minutes. Go." During the presentation, she sat as expressionless as a Mount Rushmore statue; no emotion showed. She asked for highly specific details, assessed the responses, and extended the discussion. She actually did the closing, invited me to stay longer, and settled the sale after specific responses to her time, schedule, and cost questions.

Clues to this client's style lie in her described levels of responsiveness and assertiveness. Let's analyze her behavioral style. Look first for the characteristics of responsiveness shown in Table 2-1. The words vary, but the client is fairly easy to classify as low in responsiveness. (Note her task orientation, formality, hiding of feelings, etc.) Indicate her level of responsiveness on a line that goes from low to high responsiveness in this way.

High Responsiveness

Low Responsiveness

She obviously is marked low on the line.

Table 2-1

RESPONSIVENESS DESCRIPTIONS

Low Responsiveness	High Responsiveness
Formal and Proper	Relaxed and Warm
Fact Oriented	Opinion Oriented
Guarded	Open
"Letter of the Law"	"Spirit of the Law"
Controlled	Dramatic
Disciplined About Time	Flexible About Time
Task Oriented	Relationship Oriented
Hides Personal Feelings	Shares Personal Feelings
Thinking Oriented	Feeling Oriented

Table 2-2

ASSERTIVENESS DESCRIPTIONS

Low Assertiveness	High Assertiveness
Avoids Risks	Takes Risks
Meditative Decisions	Swift Decisions
Supportive	Confronting
Easygoing	Impatient
Listens	Talks
Introverted	Extroverted
Reserves Opinion	Expresses Opinions Readily

The location of someone on this dimension is, of course, not a very precise method of evaluation; however, it gives us a start.

Now look at Table 2-2 which presents descriptions on the assertiveness dimension. Consider the lady client again. Is she high or low on an assertiveness scale? Assertiveness is harder to classify as it can be more easily controlled (more about this later). But, because the client set schedules, directed the conversation, and confronted issues, she comes out high in assertiveness, like:

Low Assertiveness   **High Assertiveness**

Put together, the ratings form a two-dimensional Responsive-Assertive Scale.

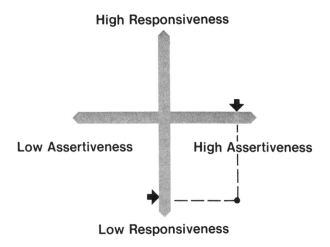

Notice where the dotted lines intersect. A single point can identify the combined effect and, therefore, can be used to categorize the client.

The next two examples give further practice in identifying levels of responsiveness and assertiveness.

Example 1

X is a businessman who exudes warmth even over the phone. He likes restaurant meetings and usually arrives early. When I arrived to meet him for the first time, he immediately got up, smiling. He called me by my first name, extended his hand to shake mine, and wrapped his left arm about my back. Asking if I liked rum and receiving a yes, he ordered a drink he was sure I'd like and recounted a story of his first encounter with the drink in New Orleans. The lunch lasted 2 1/2 hours. Fifteen minutes of this was on business, twenty minutes was on new jokes, and the rest was on X's accomplishments and interests. During the lunch, he made friends with the manager and three waitresses, including one who bumped into him as he was gesturing broadly.

How would you rate his responsiveness?

High Responsiveness

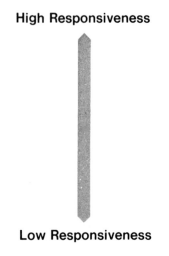

Low Responsiveness

How would you rate his assertiveness?

Low Assertiveness   **High Assertiveness**

If you identified the appropriate levels of responsiveness and assertiveness, your scales, when put together, will look like this:

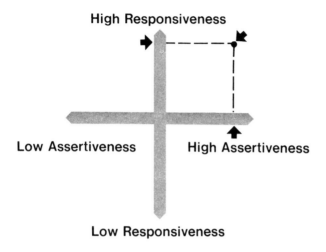

High Responsiveness

Low Assertiveness   **High Assertiveness**

Low Responsiveness

Example 2

I called a vice-president of training of a large financial institution to make a consulting arrangement. He answered his own phone in a notably quiet voice. His speed was evenly paced. Upon hearing who recommended that I call, he spent a good minute talking about his friendship with the person. His future references to me were on a first-name basis. When I asked for an appointment, he said he was flexible and asked when I could come. At our meeting, he came into the reception area and, in a soft, sure voice, greeted me by my first name. We entered the office and sat in a comfortable seating area away from the desk. He got us coffee and again described his friend who had suggested we get together. Finally, we talked about the training program. He was most concerned about the effect of the training on the communications between management and employees. He was an incredible listener. When he did ask questions, however, they tended to be tangential questions that could lead dangerously off the topic. Though I felt that he had really heard me, I walked away with an ambivalent feeling. We didn't get very far in terms of training needs. Nonetheless, we had developed a strong trust on a personal basis and parted our first meeting as friends.

How would you rate his responsiveness?

High Responsiveness

Low Responsiveness

How would you rate his assertiveness?

Low Assertiveness   **High Assertiveness**

The result is something like this:

High Responsiveness

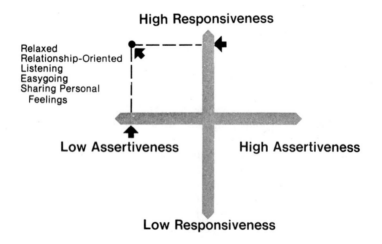

Relaxed
Relationship-Oriented
Listening
Easygoing
Sharing Personal
  Feelings

Low Assertiveness   **High Assertiveness**

Low Responsiveness

The responsive-assertive lines form quadrants which identify different, recognizable, and habitual behavior patterns — four behavioral styles: Amiable Style, Expressive Style, Analytical Style, and Driving Style. Each quadrant, therefore, represents unique combinations of responsiveness and assertiveness levels and is linked to separate and unique ways of behaving with others. Figure 2-A indicates the combined results of responsiveness-assertiveness characteristics within the four styles. The name given to each style reflects a very general characteristic rather than a full or accurate description. Although behavioral style is only a partial description of personality and character, it is highly effective in describing how others perceive a person in social and business situations. As you better understand why people behave the way they do, your knowledge can help you effectively and openly communicate with clients in a way which helps them feel more comfortable being with you.

You may have concluded that one or more of the behavioral styles are better than others. This is not true. There is no "best" behavioral style. Each style has its own unique strengths and weaknesses, and successful people as well as failures populate each style group. Figure 2-B compares the positive and negative qualities which might show up within any one style. Consider, if you will, that if others perceive your actions as appropriate and comfortable for them, they'll probably use the positive adjectives in Figure 2-B to describe you. On the other hand, if you behave with others in a way that increases tension, more than likely they will use the negative adjectives in Figure 2-B to describe you, even if your styles match.

By now, you may have identified with some of the characteristics of all four behavioral styles. That's natural. People possess traits from all four styles in varying degrees, but most people have a dominant behavioral style. It is like a theme in a musical composition. It does not describe all actions, but it is a recurring and predictable component. Like variations on the theme, people also possess traits which vary from their dominant style traits. These variations, however, can be predictable and depend upon where the person falls within a given behavioral style quadrant. So a dominant

Amiable Style

Slow at taking action and
making decisions
Likes close, personal relationships
Dislikes interpersonal conflict
Supports and "actively"
listens to others
Weak at goal-setting and
self-direction
Has excellent ability to gain
support from others
Works slowly and
cohesively with others
Seeks security and
belongingness
Good counseling skills

Expressive Style

Spontaneous actions and
decisions
Likes involvement
Dislikes being alone
Exaggerates and general-
izes
Tends to dream and get
others caught up in his
dreams
Jumps from one activity to
another
Works quickly and
excitingly with others
Seeks esteem and
belongingness
Good persuasive skills

Low Assertiveness   *High Assertiveness*

Analytical Style

Cautious actions and decisions
Likes organization and
structure
Dislikes involvement
Asks many questions about
specific details
Prefers objective, task-
oriented, intellectual
work environment
Wants to be right and,
therefore, overrelies on
data collection
Works slowly and precisely
alone
Seeks security and self-
actualization
Good problem-solving
skills

Driving Style

Decisive actions and decisions
Likes control
Dislikes inaction
Prefers maximum freedom
to manage himself and
others
Cool, independent, and
competitive with others
Low tolerance for feelings,
attitudes, and advice of
others
Works quickly and
impressively alone
Seeks esteem and self-
actualization
Good administrative skills

Low Responsiveness

Figure 2-A   Behavioral Characteristics of Each Style

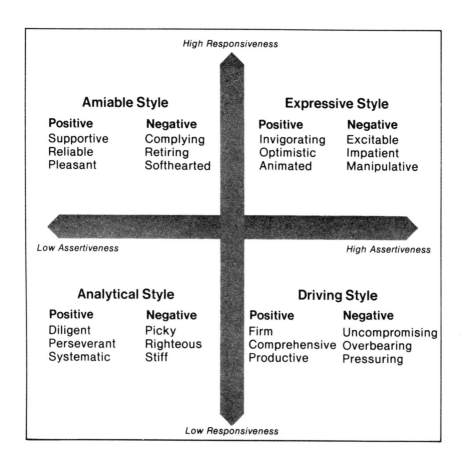

Figure 2-B   Positive-Negative Descriptions of Each Behavioral Style

behavioral style is represented by the four sections created by the two dimensions on the responsiveness-assertiveness chart. A secondary behavioral style is represented by further dividing each of the four dominant style areas into four more sections.

Now look at Figure 2-C. It presents a simple way of looking at dominant and secondary styles. For instance, look at the Driver (lower right) quadrant in Figure 2-C. As you can see, the quadrant is further divided into four "subquadrants." These subquadrants or secondary styles have the same names as the dominant quadrants. Therefore, if we divide the Driver quadrant into four equal subquadrants, the lower right subquadrant would be called

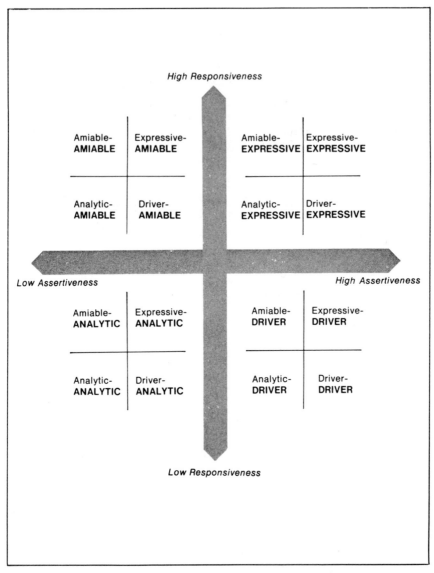

Figure 2-C Dominant Secondary Behavioral Styles

the Driver-DRIVER, the upper left subquadrant would be called the Amiable-DRIVER, and so on.

The secondary style is only a name for where a person falls within a quadrant. An Analytic-EXPRESSIVE, for instance, is first Expressive and, second, has more Analytic traits than any other Expressive. This affects the person's entire style.

The percentages on the following graph are best guesses used to show the relationship of characteristics within and across styles. The numbers suggest the percentage of time a person is in a given style or reflects those style characteristics. Only the Amiable and Expressive quadrants are shown. The traits for all other quadrants reflect a similar ranking. A dominant style will show up more heavily in an adjacent style than in a style not adjacent. This reflects pace/priority similarities, discussed next. Expressives are like Amiables in their priority; while Drivers are not similar in either pace or

AMIABLE		EXPRESSIVE	
Amiable- AMIABLE	Expressive- AMIABLE	Amiable- EXPRESSIVE	Expressive- EXPRESSIVE
AMI 70%	AMI 60%	AMI 22.5%	AMI 12.5%
EXPR 12.5%	EXPR 22.5%	EXPR 60%	EXPR 70%
DR 5%	DR 7.5%	DR 10%	DR 12.5%
AN 12.5%	AN 10%	AN 7.5%	AN 5%
Analytic- AMIABLE	Driver- AMIABLE	Analytic- EXPRESSIVE	Driver- EXPRESSIVE
AMI 60%	AMI 50%	AMI 20%	AMI 10%
EXPR 10%	EXPR 20%	EXPR 50%	EXPR 60%
DR 7.5%	DR 10%	DR 20%	DR 22.5%
AN 22.5%	AN 20%	AN 10%	AN 7.5%

priority. Therefore, Expressive characteristics show up more often in the Amiable. Note, too, that as a person is located in a quadrant closer to another primary style, the style contributes an increased number of characteristics. For instance, Driver-EXPRESSIVE is closer to the Driving Style quadrant than the Amiable-EXPRESSIVE or Expressive-EXPRESSIVE subquadrants, and the Driver characteristics tend to show up more often in Driver-EXPRESSIVE (or Analytic-EXPRESSIVE) than in the other two subquadrants.

The ability to appropriately meet the style needs of others is the key for decreasing tension, increasing trust, and being perceived positively by others. This ability is called "behavioral flexibility." We'll discuss this more fully later.

Behavioral Styles and Interpersonal Problems

Behavioral style characteristics become especially important when people of different styles meet. When that occurs and each behaves according to the characteristics of his or her own style, tension often results. I happened one day to hear two sides of the same story which point up this very issue. A salesman I knew complained of the narrow-mindedness and difficulty of a particular prospect he was trying to see. I didn't tell him I had already heard the prospect's side, but I could guess the problem.

The salesperson is an Expressive, complete with warm open handshakes, first names, and questions about client personal interests. The prospect is clearly an Analytic. I have always seen him quiet, somewhat remote (generally keeping his desk between him and others), stone-faced, and fact oriented. You can almost imagine the encounter these two had. As the salesman was involved in building a friendly relationship and dealing in general opinions and feelings, the prospect wanted to get down to business and was pressing for details.

As a result of the disastrous initial contact, the salesman thought the prospect to be picky and aloof, not interested in him or his product. The prospect thought the salesman to be uncertain of his points and intrusive in concerns that had no bearing on the business. The tension between the two was obvious, and both the prospect and the salesman had justifiable reasons for the lack of ease. None of these reasons had a thing to do with the product involved. Such increase in tension generally results in distrust, low credibility, and eventually an unproductive sales (or social) relationship.

Each style has its own unique set of priorities as to what is most important to do and each has its own pace in terms of how fast things should be done. For some, it is "I want it yesterday"; for others, "sooner or later" is acceptable. Figure 2-D relates these characteristics to behavioral styles. Notice that the Amiable and Analytic both tend to prefer a slow pace. They'll get along great as far as pace is concerned, but watch out for their priorities! Here, the Amiable does better with an Expressive. These two will still be

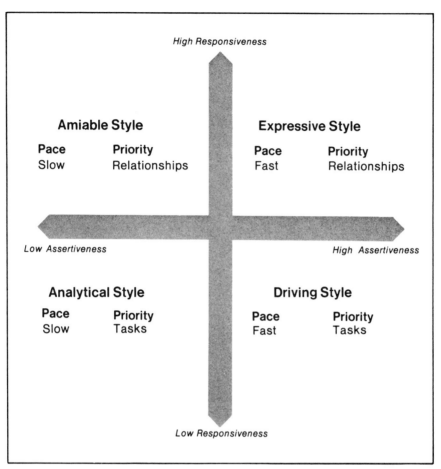

Figure 2-D   Pace and Priority of Each Behavioral Style

getting to know each other while the Analytic and Driver are already headlong into the task. The key is to know when to expect pace and priority problems and have a method to deal with them.

When the pace and priorities of two styles are not compatible, you have a problem. As you can see from Figure 2-E, the Driver-Expressive and Amiable-Analytic interactions result in priority problems. While the Driver and Analytic want to have facts and accomplish tasks to reach goals and objectives, the Expressive and Amiable want to cultivate personal relationships. The Driver and Analytic, given a choice, would begin a task without much concern for, or acknowledgment of, personal relationships. The Expressive and the Amiable, given the same choice, won't start a task until

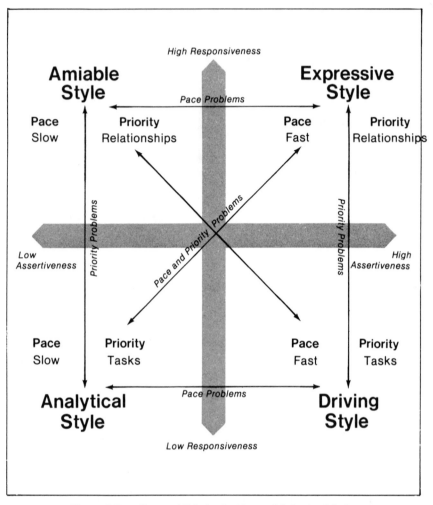

Figure 2-E   Pace and Priority Problems of Behavioral Styles

they develop the personal relationships to their satisfaction. When these pairings occur, one or the other must adjust his style to avoid increasing tension in the other. Ideally, both would move part way. For example, in the Driver-Expressive interaction, the Driver should try to show some concern for people rather than appearing to treat them as only a resource. The Expressive, on the other hand, should try to show more concern for completing the task even if the personal relationships have to be put temporarily to the side. In a sales situation, of course, the salesperson may have to make most, if not all, of that temporary adjustment.

Backup Behavior

What happens to your clients when you do not adjust your behavior to meet their style needs? Think of the salesman and prospect whose styles brought them tension and distrust in the previous example. As I reconstruct the situation, the salesman saw the prospect's questions as a personal challenge and attack to which he had to respond in order to save face. His response was to talk more and move faster, pushing the Analytic into still greater tension. By the time I spoke with the salesman, he was at the stage of attacking the prospect personally. I knew about the client's feelings only indirectly by the salesman's report of continued unsuccessful efforts to get another appointment and by the client's constantly shifting the subject away from any talk about that salesman beyond our initial remarks.

Within each individual is a point where the tension increases until it results in stress. People in stress seek to reduce the stress in any way possible. Unfortunately, most times this is unproductive. Stress is dumped on another person either verbally or psychologically. Each behavioral style has its own unproductive but characteristic manner of "dumping" stress on another. This "backup behavior" is shown in Figure 2-F.

As a rule, an Expressive (like the salesperson in our example) resorts to backup behavior by verbally attacking the person who causes the stress. And if you have an Expressive attacking, what tends to be your reaction? Most people react with increased tension of their own which, at some point, can push them into stress too. At this point, the relationship has all but ended.

The Driver under stress tends to become overbearing, pushing, uncompromising, and dictatorial. It's an outgrowth of the Driving Style: If you're hopping mad and tend to desire control and facts anyway, how would others see you at your worst? When a Driver is in backup behavior, he tends to control anyone or anything that gets in his way.

The Amiable who resorts to backup behavior generally gives in or "submits." The purpose is to avoid conflict at all costs. Although the Amiable's backup behavior on the surface may

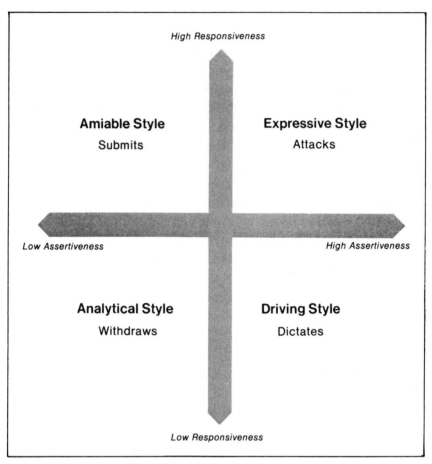

Figure 2-F   Backup Behavior Styles

appear to be a "go-along" attitude, it is certainly not that. Resentment builds because of the high tension level, and the subsequent interactions are likely to be full of distrust and tension.

Like the prospect in our last account, the Analytic's backup behavior is that of withdrawing from the other person or the situation. Being less assertive in nature, an Analytic would rather flee from the unpleasant relationship than deal with it forthright. Thus, the Analytic typically seeks more and more information and wants to think it over as a means of avoiding the other person and the unpleasant situation.

Now, think back on traditional selling and how it leads to tension and distrust in the buyer-seller relationship. The increased tension on the part of the client may exhibit itself in the form of unproductive backup behavior. Similarly, regardless of the type of selling, if the salesperson acts to reduce personal tension and disregards the style needs of the client, the client will probably experience stress and go into backup behavior. In either case, the sales relationship becomes sour, and a sale is unlikely, regardless of the needs of the client or the merits of the product or service.

To avoid backup behavior in your client, you must meet client needs, especially behavioral style needs. In short, you must treat him in a way that he wants to be treated. Not your way — his way. If he moves fast, you move fast. If he likes to take his time and get to know people, allow more time for the appointment. Move at his pace and his priority. When you meet someone's behavioral style needs, a climate of mutual trust begins to form. As that trust bond develops and strengthens, the client will begin to tell you what he really needs. He will not get into a contest with you, and you will have a more productive relationship. In addition, as you develop a better personal interaction, you will also feel better about yourself and what you are doing.

You need to accurately identify a client's behavioral style within a relatively brief time if you are to react positively and appropriately. The next section of this chapter covers this skill.

Identifying Behavioral Styles

You have some knowledge of the four types of behavioral styles and know how important it is to interact appropriately with a client's particular style. The next question... the $64,000 question... is, how do you identify which of those styles your client represents? And how do you do it fast? "Excuse me, Mr. Jones, I need to analyze your style," just won't do. Nor will it work for you to guess that the client is "supportive" or "confronting" or "guarded" or "dramatic" — or representative of these descriptive words. To identify what style your client is, you must OBSERVE WHAT THAT CLIENT DOES; you must be sensitive to both verbal and nonverbal actions. Three procedures help you quickly, accurately, and simply identify a client's behavioral style:

1. Note the client's environment.

2. Observe the client's actions.

3. Confirm your observations.

First, when you can, notice the environment in which your client works. That *may* give you some clues to the client's behavioral style. How is the office decorated and arranged? What is on the desk, walls, and bookshelf? What was the seating arrangement between you and your client? (There is still more about this specific topic in the "proxemics" section of Chapter 8.) Figure 2-G presents some of the indicators of the styles. For instance, if you entered a client's office and noticed family pictures on the desk and walls, nature posters with personal relationship motifs, a round desk, and a separate seating area with four comfortable chairs, what would be your first impression of that client's behavioral style? (Amiable) If your client then got up to greet you personally and sat with you in the easy chairs in order to discuss the purpose of your visit, would that confirm or change your initial impression? By comparing these clues against those presented in Figure 2-G, you can get a fairly good initial indication that you're indeed dealing with an Amiable.

Try another: This time you enter the office and notice:

1. Walls   A diploma; an achievement plaque; a poster that says, "Why not?"

2. Desk   Several jumbled stacks of papers piled on the desk; a chaotic appearance.

3. Seating Two overstuffed chairs and a small table close by the open side of the desk where the salesperson and client can join in a discussion.

4. Other   Bookcase with books and stacks of folders intermixed; a plant on the file cabinet.

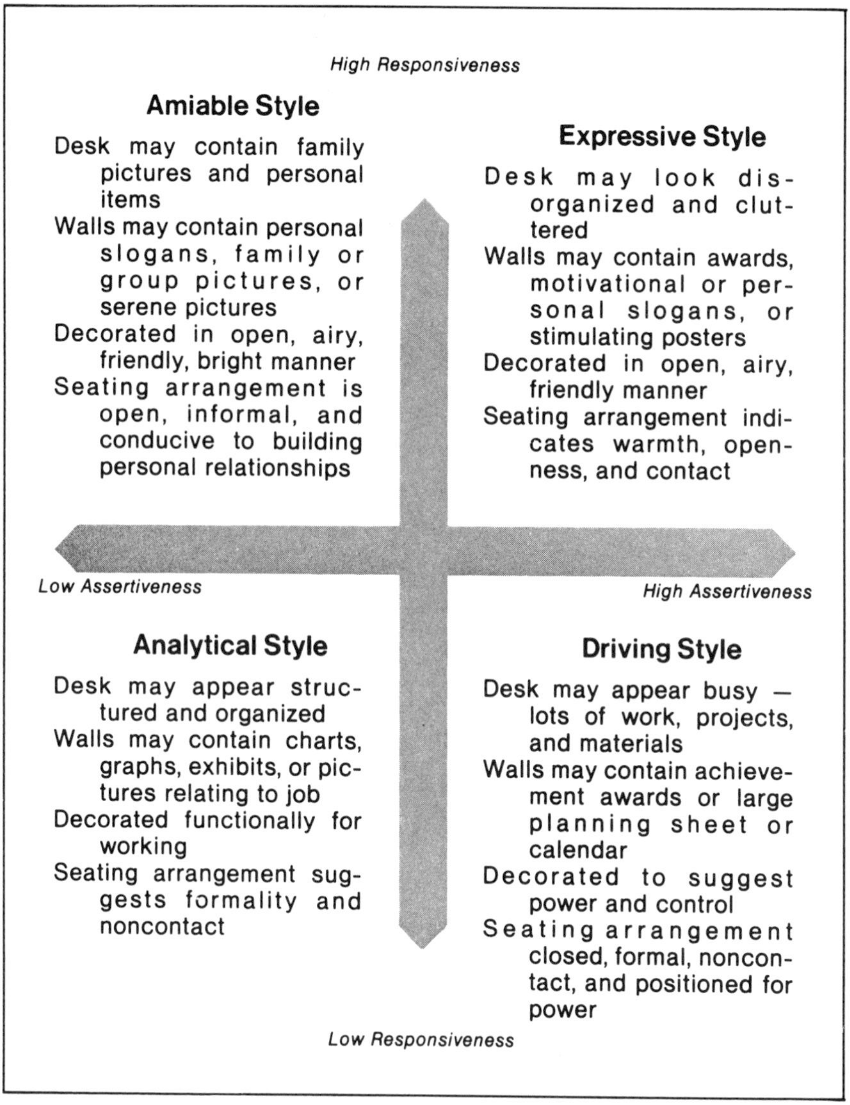

Amiable Style

Desk may contain family
pictures and personal
items

Walls may contain personal
slogans, family or
group pictures, or
serene pictures

Decorated in open, airy,
friendly, bright manner

Seating arrangement is
open, informal, and
conducive to building
personal relationships

Expressive Style

Desk may look dis-
organized and clut-
tered

Walls may contain awards,
motivational or per-
sonal slogans, or
stimulating posters

Decorated in open, airy,
friendly manner

Seating arrangement indi-
cates warmth, open-
ness, and contact

Low Assertiveness   *High Assertiveness*

Analytical Style

Desk may appear struc-
tured and organized

Walls may contain charts,
graphs, exhibits, or pic-
tures relating to job

Decorated functionally for
working

Seating arrangement sug-
gests formality and
noncontact

Driving Style

Desk may appear busy —
lots of work, projects,
and materials

Walls may contain achievement awards or large
planning sheet or
calendar

Decorated to suggest
power and control

Seating arrangement
closed, formal, noncon-
tact, and positioned for
power

Low Responsiveness

Figure 2-G   Environment Clues of Behavioral Style

Check the information in Figure 2-G. From the environment,
what kind of style does the person in that office appear to have?
(The disorganization, wall decorations of achievements and
stimulating comments of a personal nature that go beyond specific
projects, and the comfortable and accessible seating mark this as
the office of an Expressive. Get the idea?)

These environmental indicators are only one kind of clue to behavioral style. Do NOT use this as the sole determinant. Your client may have had little control over the environment you see or may have changed the environment in order to meet other needs (e.g., an intense workload, a special visitor).

The second method of identifying behavioral style is to observe it in action. This is the most crucial and accurate method. The other

OBSERVABLE RESPONSIVE BEHAVIORS

High
Responsiveness

Animated facial expressions
Much hand and body movement
Flexible time perspective
Tells stories and anecdotes
Little emphasis on facts and details
Shares personal feelings
Contact oriented
Immediate nonverbal feedback

Somewhat expressionless
Controlled and limited hand and body movement
Time disciplined
Conversation focuses on issues and tasks at hand
Pushes for facts and details
Little sharing of personal feelings
Noncontact oriented
Slow in giving nonverbal feedback, if given at all

Low
Responsiveness

Figure 2-H   Observable Responsive Behaviors

OBSERVABLE ASSERTIVE BEHAVIORS

Low Assertiveness   *High Assertiveness*

Low Assertiveness	High Assertiveness
Soft handshake	Firm handshake
Intermittent eye contact	Steady eye contact
Low quantity of verbal communication	High quantity of verbal communication
Questions tend to be for clarification, support, information	Questions tend to be rhetorical, to emphasize points, challenge information
Makes tentative statements	Makes emphatic statements
Limited gestures to support conversation	Gestures to emphasize points
Low voice volume	High voice volume
Slow voice speed	Fast voice speed
Little variation in vocal intonation	Emphasizes points through challenging voice intonation
Communicates hesitantly	Communicates readily
Slow moving	Fast moving

Figure 2-I   Observable Assertive Behaviors

two methods enhance and corroborate the "observation" technique. However, there's one catch. In order to observe someone's behavioral style, you need to observe a range of verbal and nonverbal behaviors. This may require you to stimulate more behaviors by asking questions (probes) and by "actively" listening. You can read a number of good ideas and skills for probing and listening in the communication chapters which follow.

Now to begin. Place your client at a position on both the responsiveness scale and on the assertiveness scale. To help you in positioning someone on these scales, we have translated the characteristics into a list of *observable* behaviors in Figures 2-H and 2-I. Be careful of one thing here; the behavior refers to actions you can see, not a value judgment. If you see a person hopping up and down, is he doing so because he is hop-stomping mad, stepped on a nail, has a foot that is asleep, or is extremely happy and excited? You can't tell by looking. All you can do is say he is jumping up and down. To find out *why* he is jumping requires some of the verbal and nonverbal communication skills covered in later chapters. Remember — *observable* behavior!

To identify the behavioral style using the responsive-assertive scales, first locate the client's position on the *responsiveness* dimension. It is easier to classify responsiveness behaviors quickly because they are more readily visible. Then determine the level of assertiveness demonstrated. The result is a placement of the client into one of the four behavioral style quadrants through a simple process of elimination. For instance, if you determine that your client is exhibiting higher than average responsiveness, you are automatically eliminating the styles with low responsive behavior — Driver and Analytic. Likewise, if you determine that your client is also high in assertiveness, you automatically eliminate the remaining style with low assertiveness — the Amiable. Therefore, by the process of elimination, you are left with the Expressive style for your client. Easy, isn't it? Try some examples if you wish.

These examples are from a seminar I conducted for salespeople. As you will soon see, salespeople reflect as wide a divergence of styles as any other segment of the population. Try to identify these styles.

The seminar began at 8:30 a.m. after an 8:00 coffee and doughnut session. When I arrived at 7:45 a.m., a participant was already in the room, pad and pencils neatly laid out in front of him where he sat at the table. He said nothing until I approached, and we politely shook hands. He was totally noncommittal. I asked a few questions for which I received polite, terse answers.

Around 8:15, with several other people in the room, a person stopped hesitantly at the door and softly asked, "Excuse me, am I at the training seminar for salespeople?" On being told "Yes," the person breathed a sigh, walked in, took a cup of coffee while stating how interesting the seminar would be — really helpful both in business and at home. He asked a few questions, listening intently to my remarks. He expressed some concern for role-playing in front of a group.

At this moment, another participant strode in, loudly asking, "Hey, is this the sales seminar?" On "Yes," this person dramatized a faked relief and started asking where the coffee was, explaining that he couldn't function without his "black poison." He had overheard our role-playing comments and leaped in on the conversation to say how he liked doing those things. He followed this with a tale of how he embarrassed himself in the last role-play situation in which he participated.

What would you call the style of the first gentleman described?

The second?

The third?

(We used all men in *this* set of examples. That's how it happened; however, many women attend the seminars and display equally as diverse styles.)

The first participant is clearly low in responsiveness. That means he is either an Analytic or a Driver. His low quality of conversation and restrained gestures place him as low in assertiveness — an *Analytic*. The second participant volunteered information about personal feelings and gave rapid feedback in the form of a sigh and by his comments. These are high responsiveness characteristics (Amiable or Expressive). The soft voice, questioning for clarification, and hesitance all suggest low assertiveness. This person shows an *Amiable* style. The third participant discussed is demonstrably high in responsiveness, telling stories and responding quickly. His assertiveness is also on the high side (speed of responding, fast movements, high quantity of conversation). These are *Expressive* traits.

After identifying your client's style based on environment and behavior, you should use behavioral confirmation to corroborate your choice. Behavioral confirmation is simply looking for behaviors that are characteristic of the style you believe a client represents. In other words, you have observed your client; now check this against the characteristics of the various styles. If you determined that your client is a Driver, look for specific characteristics that you expect from a Driver — competitive, impatient, efficient, decisive, fact oriented, dominant, goal oriented, and so on. If your client exhibits these types of characteristics, you have verified your choice. You can now feel comfortable in interacting with your client as a Driver. Use the same behavioral confirmation process with the other three styles. Always test and validate your initial style choice. The price for being wrong is much more severe than the time cost for confirming an initial guesstimate. Some of the more readily identifiable characteristics to help confirm each style are depicted in Figure 2-J. The list has different words from those you saw originally in Figure 2-A. This gives you a broader

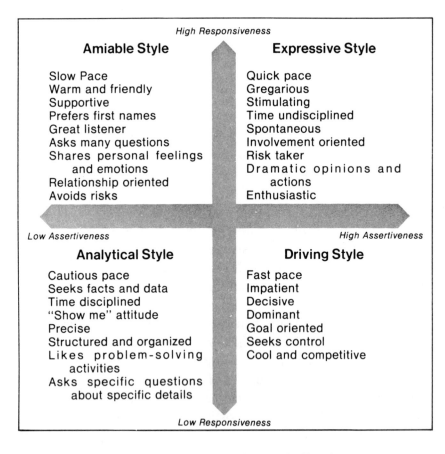

Figure 2-J   Corroborative Behavior for Each Style

way of looking at the styles. Actually, the two lists suggest the same kind of characteristics. Compare these descriptions with what you observe to simply and quickly confirm an identified behavior style.

So you've checked the environment, observed and labeled the behavioral style of a client, and confirmed your observation. You have identified your client as, let's say, a Driver, and you need to develop trust. What do you do now? You cannot expect your client to adapt to you. You need to adapt to your client. You're ready to learn communication skills to help you use this information effectively.

3

Selling Is Communicating

" "I KNOW you think you understand what I said, but I'm not
sure that what you heard is what I meant." — Sound
familiar? Have you ever had a breakdown in communication with clients when you said something that they misinterpreted
or when they said something that you misunderstood? If you can
truthfully answer "No," then I'd like to offer you a top-level job
with my company. However, if your answer is "Yes," then
welcome to the human race.

Effective "problem-solving" selling depends on efficient,
accurate communications. After all, selling is communications —
an exchange of information between you and your client. If the
information being exchanged is appropriate and accurate, you
stand to have a productive sales relationship.

This chapter discusses the general communication process. In
it, we present a communication model in order to illustrate points
at which potential problems and opportunities can occur during an
exchange of information between two people. For simplicity and
practicality, we show the communication process only from the
salesperson's perspective. That is the only part of the process
salespeople can, and should, *control*. In non-manipulative selling,

people control their own communication efforts. Of course, in successful relationships, both salesperson and client participate meaningfully in the entire two-way process.

Figure 3-A presents a model of the communication process. This model has five basic elements: It has two people, the speaker and the listener; two processes, the encoding and the decoding processes; and it has one burst of behavior, the message.

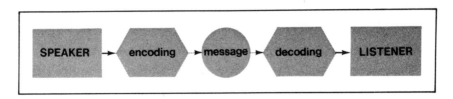

Figure 3-A   A General Model of the Communication Process

The problem faced in any communication is to get ideas from one person's head to another. Since a method for directly transferring thought has not yet been perfected, we are stuck with the problem of using an imperfect system that contains considerable opportunity for misunderstanding.

The speaker starts with "what he wants to say." He encodes this intended message into words and actions. Literally, he selects words that he thinks will convey his meaning and he throws in a variety of gestures, facial expressions, etc., that he believes will help convey his message.

The message itself involves the three Vs of communication: verbal, vocal, and visual elements. The verbal element includes the words spoken. The vocal element includes the tone and intensity of voice and other vocal qualities that are often referred to as the "music you play" with your voice. The visual elements are often the most powerful in attracting and holding a listener's attention. They include anything the speaker does that the listener can see. The message, then, is a combination of verbal, vocal, and visual elements. The listener doesn't always perceive all of these cues, and the speaker may betray an uncertain message by an inconsistency between these cues. Let's see how.

These message elements are interpreted by the listener through a process we call decoding. The listener uses his past experience, what he knows about the speaker, what he hears and sees in the message, and a whole conglomeration of things to interpret the message. In a sense, he translates the message into his own words, or what he thinks the speaker was saying.

Problems arise in three major areas. As speakers, we are not always as good as we could be in selecting words and putting them together with gestures, expressions, tone of voice, etc. How many times have you chosen the wrong word or let something that happened in the morning influence your tone of voice with some unsuspecting listener? Problems in communication also occur when the message is presented. It can be presented in the midst of many distractions or to a listener whose mind is wandering. Finally, the decoding process may cause misunderstanding. A word or a social expression may be interpreted or the listener may interpret what is said in the light of previous experience with your company, for instance.

All in all, there are places in which communication can "break down." This is especially true in selling situations. But for people who understand the communication process, miscommunication is less likely to occur, and productive communication is more likely.

Now consider a communication model for a selling situation. This is represented in Figure 3-B. The speaker becomes the seller and the listener becomes the buyer. Imagine that you are the seller.

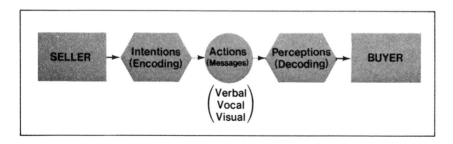

Figure 3-B   A Communication Model for Selling

As you begin the communication process with your client, you "encode" your message by putting what you intend to say into words. For accurate communication to occur, what you intend to say translates into actions that your hearer (buyer) understands. If you use words or phrases specific to your company or industry, your client may not understand what you say. Or if you use common words that can be taken several ways, your client may not take them *your* way. For instance, you might say to your client that your company provides "quick" delivery. What does that really mean? To you it might mean one week, but to your client it may mean one day. Imagine the problems that might arise if that misperception isn't corrected — soon — especially if your client is an Analytic or Driver!

As we said earlier, the actions which express your intended message include verbal, vocal, and visual elements. You want your verbal message to be understood, and generally the speaker believes that the message is carried by the meaning of the words spoken. However, listeners generally attend first to the visual and then to the vocal elements of a message, before focusing on the meaning of the words themselves.

Consider, if you will, the start of a sales meeting. You first *see* the client, and the client sees you. Imagine that you are wearing an ill-fitting wig or that your collar is partially turned under, or that you are carrying an overstuffed briefcase which looks about to burst. I dare your client to ignore the visual information and concentrate only on the meanings of your words. The visual comes first, and people respond to it before and in spite of what words may be spoken. When you or your clients do speak, the *vocal* elements are then acknowledged before the verbal meanings are attended to. If the vocal sounds are bothersome or detract in any way from the meanings of the words, people will react and understand less of what was intended. Imagine that the first sentences a salesperson speaks are in a squeaky voice, or in a monotone. What if the voice is so resonant and lovely that you are lulled by it? What if the speaker has a heavy regional or foreign accent? You *do* notice. You *do* respond. These sounds are recognized *before* you even get to the verbal meanings.

Since the visual and vocal are noticed before the verbal, you need to be *sure* they work in harmony with the verbal. You need to be alert to your visual and vocal characteristics that assist or detract from what you say.

During the message-sending process itself, numerous barriers to communication can arise. These barriers are "noise" in the communication process.

The term "noise" is used here as it is in radio communications to mean elements of the message as it is received (perceived) that get in the way of the intended message being understood. "Noise" in a selling situation can come from many sources. It may result from the seller — something said or done or worn that detracts from the message the seller is trying to send — or it may be the result of other things going on in the room, for instance, a problem that the buyer had earlier in the day. This "noise," whether internal or external interference, may actually be distracting sounds, or it may be something in your actions that disrupts the process. For instance, vocal intonations (not the intensity but the melody or sounds carrying the words) can contradict the words themselves. Has anyone ever said "No," to you while the tone of the voice said "Yes"? Either the vocal or the verbal element was "noise." "Noise" also occurs when nonverbal behavior contradicts or gets in the way of what you intend to say. For instance, the way you dress, the way you sit, the way you talk, or the way you move may create "noise" that prevents your message from being received by your client in the manner you prefer.

Your silent visual and vocal messages may speak so loudly to your client that the client may not "hear" your words. I can recall counting the times a speaker repeated the word "incredible," but I do not recall what those incredible things were. Another time I was fascinated by the manner in which a client twirled his mustache as he spoke. I walked out of his office unsure of anything actually said but with a vivid image of his mustache. Another example of visual "noise" was related by a friend of mine who spoke of an imposing, impeccably groomed young salesman who came to his office. He was so much like an ad for the rising young executive complete with leather briefcase, three-piece pinstripe suit, and black wingtip shoes, that some "noise" arose in the incongruity between the image and the nature of what he was selling. Nonetheless, he was impressive. He entered the office, sat down, crossed his legs, and lo and behold — white socks! My friend was so surprised by the flash of white at the ankles of this salesman that he could not take his eyes off the white socks. He never heard the "pitch." He never did buy from the salesman. These "noises" made it extremely difficult to hear the words. I imagine you also have concentrated your attention on someone's idiosyncrasies or method of delivery rather than the content of the message itself. Guess what? Your clients do the same with you.

The salesperson's "noise" factor modifies our model into that of Figure 3-C. Remember that both verbal and nonverbal "noise" are barriers to effective communication because they can distort the actual meaning of the message.

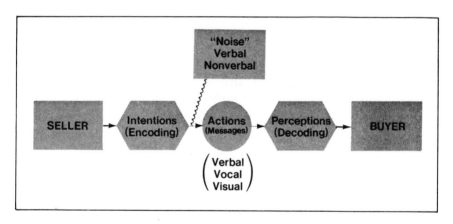

Figure 3-C   A Salesperson's Noise Factor in the Communication Model

Unfortunately, "noise" doesn't only happen when you send your message to your client. It also happens before and during the client "decoding" process, when your client perceives and interprets what he "thinks" your message meant. Client "noise" can involve actual noise, not understanding your words, or physical and mental distractions. It may be a lack of interest, daydreaming, or a host of other barriers which cause your message not to be received the way you intended. Sometimes, a client may appear not even to receive your message. Have you spoken to someone for some length of time and gotten the feeling that no one was "home"? That's "noise"! Figure 3-D includes both the salesperson's and the client's verbal and nonverbal "noise" factors. As you can see, you reach effective communication and mutual understanding only by overcoming enormous barriers — that's the bad news.

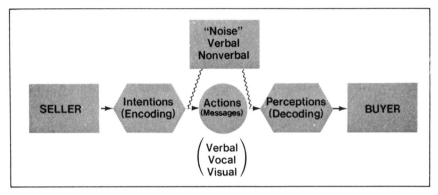

Figure 3-D   Buyer-Seller Noise Factor in the Communication Model for Selling

Now for the good news. You can get around or lessen much of the "noise." Your actions can help you say what you want in a way that gives your client a better chance to hear it. This requires the proper use of verbal, vocal, and visual skills, including feedback (skills presented in subsequent chapters). When these skills are effective, your communication is like that in the revised communication model of Figure 3-E.

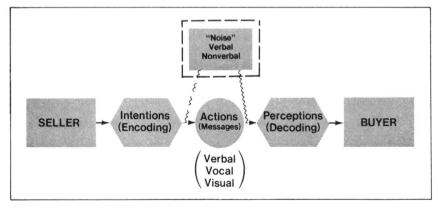

Figure 3-E   Reduced Noise for the Salesperson, Given Training in Communication Skills

At the client's end of the communication model, however, the "noise" still exists and continues to be a barrier to communication. You cannot directly control your client's "noise" as you do your own. You can, however, use the verbal, vocal, and visual skills in a FEEDBACK PROCESS to filter out and minimize client "noise" by checking how your message was received. Your verbal skills clarify *what* your client thinks you said, and your nonverbal skills "read" the client's vocal sounds and visual cues which indicate *how* that message was received by your client.

Based on the feedback, you then adjust your message in order to correct any communication errors. The feedback process and its effect on client "noise" are represented in Figure 3-F.

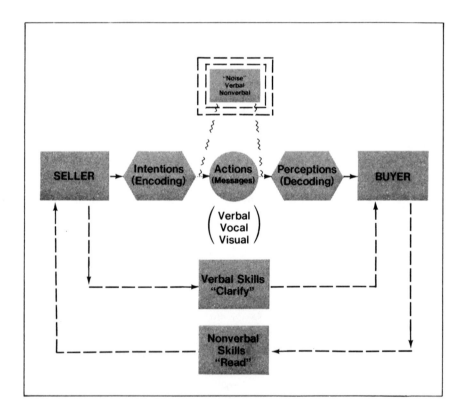

Figure 3-F   The Feedback Process and Its Effect on Buyer-Seller Noise

By using verbal and nonverbal skills during the sending and the feedback processes, you minimize communication barriers and establish an effective, efficient communication climate — a climate that establishes, maintains, and enhances mutual trust and credibility.

In the following chapters, we present specific verbal, vocal, and visual communication skills: probing, active listening, vocal intonations, image, body language, and feedback. You can then use these skills to send, listen, and give feedback to clients as you apply the specific steps of Non-Manipulative Selling.

4
The Art of Asking Questions

DO YOU ever think with envy of the salesperson who picks just the right questions to get at the core of the client's situation? Probing — asking the right questions at the right time to best help the client — is an important communication skill. Used well, probing is essential — integral — to selling. It simplifies the salesperson's job and helps increase sales. Probes help clients "open up." When a client feels free to reveal feelings or situations, motives, needs, and desires, a salesperson knows better how to help that client.

Amazingly, these essential probing skills are seldom taught. Law schools typically instruct students on productive ways to use questions within the courtroom where a witness has sworn to tell the truth, but these cases have little bearing on the world outside the courtroom where people are not obliged to answer. In the sales world, finely honed probing skills must be applied in order to obtain valid and useful information.

By skillful probing you initiate and maintain conversation to lead to a successful sales relationship. No matter whether your client is reticent to talk or leads the conversation, your probing skills help you in two specific, sales-related ways:

1. To identify client styles.

2. To uncover client needs.

In other words, a probe does more than get the client to respond.

Appropriate phrasing and content of probes promotes a good sales relationship.

Keep in mind the following general strategies as you select probes.

1. **Start with questions on broad topics and narrow with subsequent probes.** "Tell me a little about your business," is an example. If you dislike asking such a question, think for a moment of the benefits: the question gives prospects total autonomy to go wherever they wish. Clients may not present well-rounded pictures, but they will indicate areas of concern and interest to the salesperson who listens. Letting the client go where he wishes without pinning him down also acknowledges the client's expertise, for you imply that the client knows how to take the conversation in a direction meaningful to his needs. This serves to begin a trust relationship.

   The broad response opportunity also allows the client to reveal a behavioral style more readily than under a narrower probe. In other words, clients are freer to talk about goals or other concerns in their own ways. Expressives and Amiables will tend to stress a more personal connection than others (e.g., "I would like better teamwork" or "I rather like the prestige of this product"). Analytics and Drivers will tend to couch their concerns in terms of business and tasks (such as, "We need to produce more rapidly and with less waste" or "My chief concern is to track our costs better").

   You will also find that Amiables and Analytics generally will take longer to answer and be quieter in responding than Expressives and Drivers. As the client provides an answer, listen selectively for information for which you can provide help. Thus, broad questions allow responses that provide clues to client needs, problems, goals, or things that generally make the client feel good. Your ability to listen (stressed in the next chapter) will also guide you to your next question, a question which narrows your inquiry based on the client response.

   The second probe is a little narrower. It might be, "What do you do in terms of training?" or "Can you elaborate on...?" With Amiables and Expressives, try to couch this next question in terms of personal observations, human relations, or the like. With Analytics and Drivers, center on facts and details. With Amiables and Analytics, hold the pace down. Move faster with Expressives and Drivers.

Further probes follow in the same vein, moving into still narrower and more defined areas, each based on clues provided by the responses to earlier and broader probes.

2. **Keep probes free of buzz words, jargon, or technical terms that may confuse.** If a client doesn't understand the question, how can the response be accurate or complete? To avoid breakdowns in communication, carefully structure your probes to avoid confusion and promote understanding.

3. **Keep probes simple; one idea at a time is most effective.** This lets the client attend to one main subject. Probes which contain multiple ideas lead to misunderstandings. They force a client to choose between topics, and you often forget to come back to one or the other. Instead, proceed logically through each topic separately.

4. **Keep probes focused.** When the subject matter is too broad, the client's answers may be irrelevant. Notice that this deals with the *subject* matter. You still use an initially broad probe; just be in the range of the pertinent subject. When the probes wander, you may get responses far off the topic or interesting but hardly useful "war stories."

   Pursue one topic to its conclusion. That way you can more specifically help your client know why you are asking certain probes and where your probes will lead. People like to know where they are going — they dislike being led into the unknown. Imagine going to the airport and getting on a plane without knowing its destination, when it was leaving, how long it would take, or if it had enough fuel to arrive at its destination. Asking a client to go along with an unclear understanding of the logic behind your probes is similar.

5. **Keep probes nonthreatening.** Threatening probes such as, "How much money do you want to spend?" (when asked at the start of a sales interview) raise tension and decrease trust.

Other sensitive areas involve economic stability, health, age, and political affiliations. Questions in these areas may threaten your client. Moreover, your client is generally under no legal obligation to be truthful, and probes which embarrass (if answered truthfully) encourage avoidance of the truth. Therefore, despite a client's tendency toward answering honestly, be wary of answers when probes touch sensitive areas. If your client seems uncomfortable with a probe, and you don't really need the answer, move on to a different subject.

6. When questions must touch on sensitive areas, be sure to **explain why you are asking a question and indicate what the benefits are** to the client in answering forthrightly. For example, the ability to meet financial obligations is one area which may cause embarrassment for a client, yet supply crucial information. In such cases, be straightforward and businesslike. Clients respect this and usually are willing to provide necessary information. If a client hesitates at disclosing the minimal information necessary to check credit, you may be wasting time. Aside from personal questions about income and ability to meet financial obligations, queries about age and medical problems may make a client anxious and uneasy.

   If you must know about these potentially embarrassing subjects, take time to prepare your client with the rationale and phrase the questions in as nonthreatening a manner as possible. "We require our applicant to earn or have $5,000 minimum available within a week. Does that apply to you?" works a lot better than "I can't issue this until I know how much you're good for. What could you accumulate in a week?" With proper preparation, the client can anticipate the probe and be prepared to answer it. Suspicions vanish and anxieties reduce. A loan officer at a bank was told that the bank was having trouble collecting loans from underage borrowers; therefore, future applications required the person's age for processing. Faced with a middle-aged client, the loan officer said, "Mrs. Jones, the bank loan committee requires a statement of a customer's age so that we know the person is of legal age to make a loan. Some of my customers prefer to say 'twenty-one plus.' Is that all right with you?'' He received quite a few laughs, and most people just told him their age. He didn't offend clients, and he met the loan committee's need. If a client remains anxious, back off a bit, explain your purpose, and ask a second time. Be sure, however, that you need the information causing the client uneasiness. Otherwise, change to another, less threatening subject.

7. Structure probes to **ask about general benefits sought.** Probes which ask for specific features or benefits desired in a product or service can put a client on the spot. A client may very well not fully understand the needs met and problems solved by your product. To ask about general benefits allows the client to speak knowledgeably and, at the same time, gives you more latitude in satisfying needs, since general benefits are easier to provide than specific features. Consider two people selling real estate. One tries to solve client problems by asking specifics early in the sales relationship, such as ''Do you want a fireplace?'' The other keeps the probe more general: ''Do you like a romantic feeling in your home?'' What's the implication? Note that if the first one cannot show a house with a fireplace, an awkward situation exists unless the client's needs are renegotiated. The second salesperson maintains wide latitude: a fireplace, a cozy corner, a den, a patio, a pool, and so on. The more general request will not limit or terminate the sale too early in the sales relationship.

8. Phrase probes so as to **allow a client to answer rather than forcing an answer.** ''How do your mornings look for an appointment this week?'' is better than, ''Would you prefer to see me at 10:00 a.m. on Tuesday or 8:30 a.m. on Thursday?'' The latter is manipulative; and manipulation, even if unintended, violates the client's sense of dignity and insults client intelligence.

9. **Maintain a consultative atmosphere** as you probe. You are an assistant to your client, not an attorney with the client on the witness stand. Interrogative, rapid-fire questions won't pressure your client into answering — at least not over the long (and sales-prosperous) haul. Use a relaxed tone of voice. Give your client time to contemplate the probe, even if it means a

period of silence. By pausing and allowing time to think, you will likely receive a more accurate and complete reply. Do not interrupt. Proceed only after the answer is complete.

10. **Phrase probes so they are easy to answer.** Research has shown that people prefer to agree to something rather than to voice objections. Therefore, if you sense your client has a preference, phrase your question to allow for this preference to come through. Say, "Would you like the small size?" (that being the case) rather than, "Would you like the large size?" The hypothesis is that the client tends to answer the probe in the easiest manner possible. It is easier to agree to the small size by saying "Yes," than to specify objections to the larger size.

    As you probe, be careful that easy-to-answer questions are what you *want*. Some questions, called closed-ended, are easy to answer in that they require only a yes or no or some other short reply. That quickly terminates a flow of conversation when used inappropriately.

11. Finally, **phrase your probes in light of the perceived behavioral style of your client**, thereby minimizing tension while gathering necessary information. For Expressives and Amiables, concentrate more on probes about feelings and opinions: "How do you feel about...?" or "What is your opinion on...?" Avoid these for Analytics and Drivers. Instead, stress fact oriented and thinking oriented probes such as, "What do you think about...?" or "Based on the fact, what...?" Probes structured around the behavioral styles of your clients allow a comfortable and natural way for clients to give and receive information.

Types of Probes

After the preliminary "how-do-you-do's" and other easy conversation openers, the real probing begins. Once you know your probing strategies, you still have to decide how to phrase probes to promote the strategies. A properly selected and phrased probe can dramatically further your client's and your own relationship. Below are some guidelines to this selection.

Probes take on two basic forms: OPEN END and CLOSED END.

I. OPEN END

Open end probes are phrased to draw out a wide range of responses on a broad topic. They attempt to involve the client by asking for knowledge of a subject (asked, for instance, of an Analytic or Driver) or by asking for opinions about a topic (asked, for instance, of an Amiable or Expressive). Examples of open end probes are:

"What type of billing schedule would meet your needs best?"

"What kind of features do you like on your TV set?"

These probes usually have the following characteristics:

1. They cannot be answered by a simple yes or no.

2. They usually begin with "what" or "how."

3. They do not lead the client in a specified direction.

4. They increase dialogue by drawing out the client's ideas or feelings.

5. They encourage the client to elaborate on objectives, needs, wants, and problems.

6. They help the client to discover things for himself or herself.

7. They can be used to stimulate the client into thinking about your ideas and product or service.

8. They allow the client to exhibit his or her behavioral style more readily than closed questions.

II. CLOSED END

Closed end probes require narrow answers to a specific inquiry. The answers to these questions are typically yes, no, or some other very brief answer. Examples of closed end probes are:

"Does the monthly billing schedule meet your needs?"

"Is having remote tuning on a TV set important to you?"

Probes of this nature perform the following functions:

1. They allow specific facts to be obtained.

2. They are simple to answer in that clients only need to answer one question, so long as they have been adequately prepared for the probe.

3. They are useful in the feedback process where the salesperson desires to check the communication accuracy or completeness.

4. They may be used to gain commitment to a definite position.

5. They can be used to reinforce positive statements.

6. They can be used to direct the conversation to a desired topic or concern.

Whether or not a probe is closed or open end, it can serve several functions, depending on how it is stated. Some of the more generally used types follow.

Clarifying Probes

Clarifying probes restate the client's remarks or refer directly to them. They generally are accompanied by a rising inflection in the voice which implies a question, even if one is not directly asked. "So, you will be here on Tuesday," is a statement, but with a rising inflection implies the additional "Isn't that so?" These probes do not insist that what was heard and included in the probe was what the client actually said. Rather, they feed back what you understood by the client's remark. Examples of these probes are:

"If I hear you right, you're saying that you need at least one copy for each secretary. Is that so?"

"Are you speaking about peripherals or just the central processing unit?"

These probes may be successfully used to:

1. Express in different words what the client appears to have meant. This is to check your understanding.

2. Invite the client to expand or clarify an idea previously expressed.

3. Help clarify ambiguities and broad generalizations.

4. Uncover what is on the mind of the client.

Developmental Probes

Developmental probes ask for further information from the client on a subject already introduced. They are designed to draw out a wide range of responses on an identified topic. Examples of developmental probes are:

> "You mentioned needed repair. Do you recall what kind of problems resulted in your calling a repairman?"

> "We have quite a few homes that have room for family activities. Tell me, what does each member of your family like to do in or around the house?"

Notice that the fairly narrow topics, repair problems and family-related activities, are open to a relatively unpredictable and long list of responses. Developmental probes help in the following ways:

1. They ask for additional information in a more detailed form.

2. They encourage the client to expand and elaborate upon the topic being pursued.

Leading Probes

Leading probes imply their own answers. When used to guide the client into a better understanding of his or her own needs, they are acceptable tools in the problem-solving process. Some traditional sales trainers advocate the use of leading probes to manipulate the client into a commitment. You may be familiar with the ploy involved in the question, "Which color do you like best?" followed with artificial choices to get the client to feel he has selected the product. The sophisticated buyer is aware of such tactics, and manipulation with this sort of leading probe generally ruins the trust and sales relationship. Well used leading probes help:

1. Direct the conversation and sales presentation through logical steps. ("As you see here, what is the third step?")

2. Provide a means of supplying necessary information to the client. ("From my viewpoint, I see three conditions for us to have a successful relationship: good quality products with service to back them up, fair and reasonable prices, and assurance that the delivery dates can be met. Do you agree?")

3. Give the client an additional way to participate in the information exchange. ("Many people in your industry, for example, Mr. Whei, have found that using this product has saved them money. Do you think this product will save you money?")

Assumptive Probes

The assumptive probe is another effective tool that requires careful use. This kind of probe includes an assumption asked in question form. Timing and sensitivity in reading the client are important on the salesperson's part if the assumptive probe is to be well used. Otherwise, it is seen as a "trap" to force a decision, and thereby reduces the credibility of the salesperson using it. The assumptive probe can be helpful, though, in the following ways:

1. It can check for understanding. ("Did you want delivery as early as next week?" Here, it assumes that delivery is to be provided and is checking when.)

2. It can help the client finalize decisions. ("When shall we have our initial consulting seminar?")

Third Party Opinion Probes

Third party opinion probes combine a statement and a probe. They probe indirectly by relating to the client how others feel or react to a particular subject. They then ask the client to give his opinions and reactions concerning the same subject. Research indicates a greater acceptance of a statement if a well-known and respected person or corporation endorses that statement, so long as the mention isn't perceived as name-dropping. Third party opinion probes, therefore, are used to:

1. Increase client confidence in the way problems or needs can be responded to by suggesting that others of name or note have solved a similar need in a similar way. (*"Consumer's Union* has rated this product as the best available for its price range. Is this the price range you're interested in?")

2. Increase client pride in a decision or perception. ("That's a good selection. Mr. Jay at Beeu Manufacturing, the president of the national manufacturers' group, has used this product successfully to cut his downtime by 30 percent. Do you have similar downtime considerations?")

In summary, probing skills are most effective with the right probes used at the right time for the right purpose. Accomplishing this, of course, hinges on a solid understanding of the product or service being offered and on the conditions the client faces which make a product or service attractive, even necessary. Then probing strategies are built on this foundation — strategies that lead to uncovering and solving client needs in the shortest, least threatening manner.

5

Listening Your Way to More Sales

RECENTLY, THE National Society of Sales Training Executives conducted a survey among purchasing agents throughout the United States to determine what those agents perceived to be the major shortcomings in today's salespeople. In terms of selling skills, the number one shortcoming was listening.

If selling involves information exchange, then it cannot be one way; listening is, by definition, part of the process. Clients provide information about problems in exchange for information about potential solutions. Not to listen effectively to a client has at least two detrimental effects. First, solutions tend to be faulty or inappropriate. If you don't listen fully to your client's problems, how can you effectively present solutions? Second, a client is likely to turn the tables and not listen to you. In contrast to these are the cooperation and understanding that arise through "active listening."

Unfortunately, however, listening skills are very often ignored or just forgotten in sales training. While businesses may be willing to spend the money to send executives to sales courses, they rarely direct personnel to courses designed to improve listening habits, even though effective salespeople spend the majority of their sales time listening. The reason for this may be due to the misconception, held by many, that listening is the same as hearing and everybody does it. This is just not so. Nichols and Stevens, in their book *Are You Listening?*, point out that a person listens with about a 50 percent efficiency and that information loss is compounded as the message is passed from person to person. In other words, people may hear an entire message and still lose or distort meaning. It is much like the childhood game of passing a sentence verbally from person to person around a room. The fun results when the last person to receive the sentence repeats it aloud and compares it with the original message. The two messages may not even be in the same language anymore. Without adequate listening skills, what is understood is not necessarily what has been said.

In fact, while the normal, untrained listener is likely to understand and retain only about 50 percent of a conversation, this relatively poor percentage drops to an even less impressive 25 percent retention rate 48 hours later. Think of the implications. Memory of a conversation which took place more than two days ago will always be incomplete and usually inaccurate. No wonder people can seldom agree about what has been discussed!

Effective listening is hard work. It not only involves considerable concentration, it even causes noticeable physical changes. During "active listening," heart action increases, body temperature rises slightly, and the circulation of blood is faster. You can actually learn to sense these changes in yourself just by being aware that they occur when you are actively listening to someone.

The focus of this chapter is on skills you can use to actively listen to clients. It also presents ways to avoid misunderstanding or irritating your clients through ineffective listening habits. The net result of this chapter, if you implement its ideas and suggestions, is that your clients will feel understood, feel good about you, and sense that you listen to them. Moreover, when you listen to someone, that person tends to work harder at listening to what you have to say, too.

Levels of Listening

Whenever people listen, they are at one of three basic levels of listening or attentiveness. Each requires a particular depth of concentration on the part of the listener. As you move from the first to the second to the third level, the potential for understanding and communication increases.

Marginal Listening

Client: What I need, really, is a way to reduce time lost due to equipment breakdowns.

Salesperson: Yeah, OK. Let's see, uh, the third feature of our product is the convenient sizes you can get. (I wonder if I can get my plane reservations.)

Marginal listening, the first level, involves the least concentration and attention. The listener is easily distracted by his or her own thinking and fleeting impressions. During periods of marginal listening, a listener will exhibit blank stares, nervous mannerisms, and gestures that tend to annoy the client and cause communication barriers. The message is toyed with but not really heard. For this reason, marginal listening is the most dangerous of the three levels. There is enormous room for misunderstanding when a salesperson is not concentrating on what is being said. Moreover, the client cannot help but feel the lack of attention. Think of the insult and the diminishing trust bond. It is funny in comedy when family members continually respond to each other with, "Yes, dear." It is not funny in real life.

Marginal listening can occur in salespeople of all experience ranges. Salespeople who are unsure of themselves and lack confidence and experience can concentrate so hard on what they are supposed to say next that they stop listening. On the other hand, the "old pro" has heard it all before, has his presentation memorized, and wants the client to hurry up and finish so the "important" business can continue. Of course, the truly important information lies in what the client is saying.

Evaluative Listening

Client: What I need, really, is a way to reduce time lost due to equipment breakdowns.

Salesperson: (defensively) We have tested our machines in the field, and they don't break down often.

Evaluative listening, the second level of listening, requires somewhat more concentration and attention to the speaker's words. At this level, you are actively trying to hear what the client is saying, but you aren't making an effort to understand your client's intent. Instead of accepting and trying to understand a client's message, the evaluative listener categorizes the overall argument (or statement) and concentrates on preparing a response. The speaker in our example obviously has had some experience with breakdowns. This indicates an area the salesperson should pursue to discover the nature and type of breakdowns involved.

The evaluative listening phenomenon is a result of the tremendous speed at which a human can listen and think. While a person speaks at an average rate of 120 to 160 words a minute, the mind is capable of listening and thinking up to four times this speed. No wonder evaluative listening is the level of listening that we employ the most in everyday conversations. It establishes a very difficult habit to break.

Of course, evaluative listening greatly speeds up sales conversations. The salesperson anticipates the client's words and is ready with a response almost as soon as the client finishes speaking. The concentration of the evaluative listener, however, is misplaced; and the results are potentially dangerous to the sales relationship (and, therefore, to the sales).

Most of the salesperson's attention is on a response, whether it is an agreement or a rebuttal. Therefore, an evaluative listener forms opinions about the client's words before the message is complete and risks not accurately understanding the message being sent. Furthermore, the excess time provided by the speed with which the mind works promotes distractions if attention is not fully channeled to listening. Then the opportunity arises for highly emotional words to arouse emotion or distraction in the listener, who may then concentrate entirely on an examination and possible rebuttal of the client's emotional remarks. This is especially true when the comments run counter to the listener's style needs, as when an Amiable client complains that a Driver salesperson failed to provide enough personal attention. The Driver finds this people-related concern hard to understand and may spend a great deal of time thinking up rebuttals instead of trying to believe the complaint and act on the problem. As a result, backup behavior often results, and the trust bond is lost.

Active Listening

> Client: What I need, really, is a way to reduce time lost due to equipment breakdowns.
>
> Salesperson: Could you tell me what kind of breakdowns you have experienced and in what way you need to have them handled more effectively?

Active listening is the third and most effective level of listening. The active listener refrains from evaluating the client's message and tries to see the client's point of view. Attention is not only on words spoken, but also on the thoughts and feelings of the client. To listen in this manner requires a suspension of personal thoughts and feelings in order to give attention solely to listening. It means figuratively "putting yourself into someone else's shoes." It also requires the listener both verbally and nonverbally to indicate to the client that what the client is saying is really being absorbed.

As mentioned, listening in this manner is tiring. It takes great concentration. However, if you really want to develop the skill of listening, you must attain this power of attention. Some exercises help improve this concentration level.

One such exercise involves interpreting, in your own words, your understanding of the speaker's message before giving a reply. You might practice using clarifying probes here to check your understanding. Your interpretation of the speaker's message has to meet the intended meaning to the speaker's satisfaction before you are able to voice your own message. This exercise requires a patient, understanding friend. It will slow conversation to a snail's pace, but it will certainly point out the amount of misunderstanding that infiltrates conversations and how it breaks down communication.

For another exercise, find a tape recording of a speech or conversation. Then use a timer to mark (audibly) a three-minute interval (or five, if you're daring) during which you concentrate on the message as if the speaker were your client. When the timer goes off, stop the tape and note everything you can remember being said — not just the main points. Play back the tape for any surprises, and practice until you eliminate these surprises.

Guidelines for Active Listening

Being a good listener involves applying rules of courtesy and common sense — and a bit more. Rudeness is rarely intended, but enthusiasm for a subject and personal desire to get things moving often override courtesy. Sometimes, too, salespeople are so intent with their own point of view that they simply forget to listen to what the client is saying.

Good relations between you and your client develop over a period of time, and listening plays an important part in that successful development. By listening to client problems and needs, you have been taken into confidence; and that confidence requires an understanding on the salesperson's part that translates into action. As you act to help the client solve dilemmas and to positively effect the client's goals, you solidify the relationship — the trust.

Listening is a skill which the following guidelines are designed to help develop. They are centered in four areas of concern:

    A. Listen to the client.
    B. Reduce and circumvent "noise."
    C. Organize the message you hear.
    D. Check your listening.

A. LISTEN TO THE CLIENT

1. Let the client talk.

When an important person speaks, you listen. In sales, the most important person is the client. Wait for the client to finish speaking, and then respond to what has been said. Interrupting a client's comments or rapid-firing statements during a pause in the client's statement is not only a possible irritation, it actually slows conversations; for the client must keep trying to regain the train of thought. The only interruption a person likes is applause. A client will accept this form of assent and approval with a smile. Even so, the stream of thought may be lost. Nods and smiles of encouragement are accepted and helpful when not overdone.

Given the chance to speak uninterrupted, the client may reveal interesting facts and valuable clues to aid you in helping solve problems or satisfy needs — facts and clues which an interruption may have cut short. As the client reveals interests, you can tailor your sales presentation to fit that client's particular needs. You can dispense with those aspects of the presentation which are inappropriate for that client at that point in time. This benefit is probably a great contributor to the success of salespeople who are careful listeners. They are better able to pick up and use clues to client needs that their evaluative listener counterparts miss.

By encouraging the client to talk and take an active part in the sales presentation, he may end up "selling himself." He may solve his own problems by just talking about them with you. He may even come up with some product benefits that you hadn't thought of before. In addition, being encouraged to talk allows the client personal autonomy and keeps him from feeling pressured into a sale. By building confidence and reducing tension, the trust bond between you and your client is strengthened. A client who "sells himself" is likely to be more fully committed and less likely to have "buyer's remorse." He will likely become a staunch defender of your product, be open-minded with you in future dealings, and be more likely to reciprocate in listening to you.

Besides helping you develop an effective trust bond with your client, allowing your client to talk can aid in keeping up the interest in the sales discussion. Outside distractions always threaten to draw attention away from a conversation. So, by encouraging the client to participate, you have a better chance of retaining a high level of attention. After all, the person doing the talking is always interested in what is said. It isn't the lecturer who falls asleep!

2. Listen for client psychological needs.

As you center your interest on the client, be awake not only to product but also to psychological needs. Product needs are often the only concern in a sales discussion, for both client and salesperson are ready to discuss them. However, psychological needs do exist, and the salesperson who can identify them will be better able to help the client in the way the client wishes to be helped. These psychological needs are subtle and more difficult to define, as they are internal to the client. With careful listening, you will hear reasons behind the selection of a product or service. Some clients may react to the packaging; others to product prestige; others to efficiency capabilities or other performance features. The client buys not just a product or service, but a reflection and comment upon the person behind the choice — the client. We all know the difference in the statements a Porsche and Cadillac make about the driver. Both products are in the same price ranges and both project wealth; however, one also projects a liberal, flamboyant personality and the other a conservative, steady personality.

Another kind of psychological need lies within the sales situation itself. It has to do with client-salesperson relationships. Some clients thrive on reassurance; others have a strong need to be supported. All wish to feel understood. Clients feel relieved when they find a salesperson who understands what they have to say about their problems. This is one of the reasons they buy from a particular salesperson. Understanding the client is a cornerstone in the non-manipulative selling philosophy. Become sensitive to the client's use of personal pronouns (I and we) because these signal particular areas and subjects which are of interest to that particular client. Make a conscious effort to focus on the client's needs by emphasizing pronouns like "you" and "your."

B. REDUCE AND CIRCUMVENT NOISE

1. Listen attentively.

Listen attentively and let your client know that you are. When possible, try to ensure an atmosphere of privacy that avoids external distractions. Face your client squarely with uncrossed arms and legs, and lean slightly forward in a relaxed posture. Establish good eye contact. Use affirmative head nods where appropriate, but not to the point of overdoing them. Let your entire body "say" that you are at ease and interested.

Intermittently acknowledge your client's message with "uh-hum," "I see," "I understand," "yes-s-s," or other appropriate and nonintrusive remarks.

Developmental and clarifying probes also indicate attention and invite your client to concur or correct and then to continue or elaborate. Phrases like "Tell me more about that," "Can you give me an example?" or "Then what?" indicate strong interest in what your client is saying.

2. Minimize the impact of distractions.

Train yourself to listen carefully to your client's words despite interruptions. Distractions may be external to the conversation, such as a ringing telephone or other office noise. Particularly insidious, however, is the effect of internal distractions on the sales environment. You cannot control the client's internal noise, but you can do a lot to control your own. Mainly, you need to be aware of them. One kind of internal distraction is the effect that client idiosyncrasies have upon you. If something about the client's speech or image or mannerisms is attracting your attention, deal with it by forcing yourself to concentrate still more on the message. Some helpful guidelines follow in the next section. Focus attention solely on the words, ideas, feelings, and cues to the underlying intent of your client.

Another kind of internal distraction is that caused by emotional deaf spots. Deaf spots are caused by words or actions which make your mind wander. Once you hear or see them, you no longer hear the speaker. Everyone is affected by this now and then. Try to discover your individual stumbling blocks and prepare to deal with them. When client idiosyncrasies bother you, plan ways to involve yourself more actively with getting the message whenever you feel your concentration slipping.

Finally, try to remain relaxed and removed from extreme emotions. Emotions of any kind hinder listening (remember the last time you laughed and had to struggle to get back on the track?). Anger, however, is a particularly detrimental emotion to communication. When a word or idea triggers anger, logical thinking is lost. A good listener puts aside strong emotions as best he can so as to be open to the entire message.

C. ORGANIZE THE MESSAGE YOU HEAR

This involves true listening. It does not mean to imply "evaluative" listening where the listener selects the content.

1. Take notes.

Do not trust memory when facts and data are important — take notes, but make sure you ask your client's permission before doing so. Use phrases and key words to indicate pros and cons of arguments rather than writing complete thoughts. All you need is reminder phrases to jog your memory. Read and review your notes as you have time to be sure they make sense to you. Always be sure to review the notes again before subsequent contacts with your client

2. Listen to all.

Your role is that of a sounding board for your clients. Try to understand your clients without making value judgments. Understand with them, not about them. This means that you take a sincere interest in everything your client has to say. Do not listen only for what you want to hear. What the client is interested in saying gives you clues to his or her motivations, needs, and feelings. As you do this, be selective in terms of identifying specifically what your client is telling you that can assist you in meeting his or her needs and solving his or her problems.

3. Identify main and supportive points in the client's message.

Listen for your client's main ideas. As you do this, identify, also, those points made in support of the ideas. Specific facts and examples are important only as they relate to the main themes, and they can cause misunderstandings if taken out of context. Take advantage of pauses to review portions of the discussion that have already been covered (using good probes). Ask yourself, "What is his point?" or "What is this getting at?" If you guess correctly, your understanding and retention increase. If you are incorrect, you will have time to correct your outline and be alert to judgments or assumptions that you may have subconsciously and incorrectly made.

4. Support and reinforce any of your client's statements that lead toward the solution of an identified problem.

As you identify what your client is most interested in, you also identify which of the details or ideas can be aided by your product and service. React visibly (attentively) to your client when these subjects are broached. You both are on a troubleshooting, goal-hunting expedition and need to center on ways to be successful. Help the client do this by identifying steps toward a solution.

5. Listen "between" the words.

Unless listening is coupled with other skills, it can mislead you. What is said may not be what that client means. He may say he likes a product, but — there's something wrong; you know that he doesn't like it all that much. How do you know? Sixth sense? We prefer to call it "listening between the words." Learning to read those subtle (sometimes not-so-subtle) signals that speak more honestly than the words saves many a salesperson from improper sales advice.

Each individual has a unique way of nonverbally expressing mood and attitude changes, and a good listener will strive to understand all these cues. The communication of these unspoken thoughts and feelings can be recognized, when incongruent with the verbal, through eye contact wherein changes of mood are expressed. Watch, too, for changes in the sound of the voice, speaking pace, breathing, facial expressions, posture, body movement, and many more observable aspects of your client.

In trying to interpret nonverbal cues, listen for total meaning. In other words, the verbal meaning is not enough, and visual and vocal cues provide powerful sources of information. Your ears allow you to hear the content, but both your ears and eyes aid you in interpreting and understanding the feelings and actions underlying the client's actual words. Use all your senses. The sections on vocal intonation, image, and body language give additional ways for you to fully "listen" to the client.

D. CHECK YOUR LISTENING

Remember the feedback loop in the communication model of Chapter Three? Here's the chance to use it to further reduce "noise." The following questions and concerns, if applied to each sales situation, will help you check the accuracy and completeness of the communication.

- Do you understand the speaker's words in the speaker's way?

- Do you restate the ideas accurately? (For this, use clarifying questions. As you do this, you will also demonstrate to your client that you are truly interested in understanding the message. Use phrases such as, "Do I hear you saying...?" "I understand your major concern to be..." or "...Is that correct?"

- Can you pinpoint the speaker's assumptions and compare them with your own?

- Can you determine the speaker's information source? Is it experience, observation, or opinion?

- Does the message make sense when taken in context with the entire conversation? If not, can you explain the inconsistency?

Consistently check to see if your client wants to comment on, or respond to, anything you have said. This request for feedback on a broader range, allows the client a chance to clarify or expand ideas of which you may otherwise remain ignorant. It also reduces the tension that arises when a client feels his or her message is not truly understood, despite the apparent satisfaction of the salesperson.

Irritating Listening Habits

The listening strategies are meant to help you foster a free-flow, open communication climate with your clients. On the other hand are listening habits which irritate clients and tend to erect barriers to effective information exchange. The following list presents nearly two dozen of these. As you review the list, you may wish to identify which of the guidelines is being betrayed. Also, as you read, try to honestly identify any habits you have. If you find any (and you probably will), work quickly on overcoming them in order to fully implement your active listening habits.

For your benefit, the letter and number used in the text for each guideline appears after any example which is inconsistent with that guideline. These guidelines are reviewed here for ease of reference.

Review of Guidelines to Good Listening

A. Listen to the Client
   1. Let the client talk.
   2. Listen for client psychological needs.

B. Reduce and Circumvent "Noise"
   1. Listen attentively.
   2. Minimize the impact of distractions.

C. Organize the Message You Hear
   1. Take notes.
   2. Listen to all.
   3. Identify main and supportive points in the client's message.
   4. Support and reinforce any of your client's statements that lead toward the solution of the identified problem.
   5. Listen "between" the words.

D. Check Your Listening

IRRITATING LISTENING HABITS

1. He does all the talking; I go in with a problem and never get a chance to open my mouth. (A.1, A.2)

2. He interrupts me when I talk. (A.1, A.2)

3. He never looks at me when I talk. I'm not sure he's listening. (B.1)

4. He continually toys with a pencil, paper, or some other item while I'm talking; I wonder if he's listening. (B.1, B.2)

5. His poker face keeps me guessing whether he understands me or is even listening to me. (C.4, D)

6. He never smiles — I'm afraid to talk to him. (C.4)

7. He changes what I say by putting words into my mouth that I didn't mean. (C.1, C.3, C.4)

8. He puts me on the defensive when I ask a question. (C.2, D)

9. Occasionally he asks a question about what I have just told him that shows he wasn't listening. (B.1, B.2)

10. He argues with everything I say — even before I have a chance to finish my case. (A.1)

11. Everything I say reminds him of an experience he's either had or heard of. I get frustrated when he interrupts, saying "That reminds me..." (A.1, B.1, C.4)

12. When I am talking, he finishes sentences for me. (A.1)

13. He acts as if he is just waiting for me to finish so he can interject something of his own. (A.1, B.1)

14. All the time I'm talking, he's looking out the window. (B.1)

15. He looks at me as if he is trying to stare me down. (C.4)

16. He looks as if he's appraising me... I begin to wonder if I have a smudge on my face, a tear in my coat, etc. (B.2, C.4)

17. He looks as if he is constantly thinking "No" or questioning the truthfulness or value of what I'm saying. (B.1, C.4)

18. He overdoes showing he's following what I'm saying... too many nods of his head, or mm-hm's, and uh-huh's. (C.3, C.5)

19. He sits too close to me. (B.2)

20. He frequently looks at his watch or the clock while I am talking. (B.1, B.2)

21. He is completely withdrawn and distant when I'm talking. (B.1, C.4)

22. He acts as if he is doing me a favor in seeing me. (B.2, C.1, C.4)

23. He acts as if he knows it all, frequently relating incidents in which he was the hero. (A.1, B.1)

In Summary

Learning to listen effectively pays off in stronger trust bonds and increased sales. Clients feel relieved to find salespeople who actively listen and understand what they have to say about their problems and needs. Once that occurs, clients generally reciprocate by listening to the salesperson and trying to understand why a particular product or service will meet their needs. That leads to an open, honest information exchange between client and salesperson. Isn't that what (non-manipulative) selling is all about?

6

It's Not WHAT You Say...
It's HOW You Say It

I USED to know someone in public relations who would avoid the wrath of parents by looking at their child and saying, "Now, *there* is a baby." Comparable statements are, "You *do* have a product," "That *is* an idea." Notice that the *words* (verbal meanings) are noncommittal. If the baby is ugly, the product bad, or the idea suspect, the person hasn't lied — by the words. The departure from truth comes in the *sound* of the words — that part of the message which is lost when speech is written rather than spoken — the sum effect of the vocal qualities. Now, we don't advocate lying; but the examples above do point up the power of this additional way of adding meaning. Every sentence you speak is uttered with sounds that by their speed, relative stress, volume, and rhythms say as much or more than the words themselves. Knowledge of how this works will help you listen to your client better and indicate ways to say what you wish to say with greater impact.

Getting Information from Vocal Qualities

You have always picked up some information from the sound of another's voice. High emotions (joy, anger, affection, and the like) come across as readily in the sound as in other visual and verbal (word-meaning) cues. Think about the difference in the voices of the angry mother and the lonely husband saying, "Susie, come here." Many of us have talked with someone on the phone and known that person was really angry, even when the words were in themselves fairly matter-of-fact. You already know how to recognize these cues. However, you can learn — or further develop an ability — to read cues in vocal qualities that are far more subtle. Then you can act to encourage or circumvent a change in attitude or thinking before the emotion gets high or the change in idea becomes entrenched.

The steps for obtaining information from vocal qualities are deceptive in that they are simple; but as with so many skills, they seem awkward or unimportant to use at first and take on power as you apply them repeatedly. Two steps are involved:

1. **Identify the client's characteristic vocal qualities.**

    What is characteristic for one person is not for another. If you think back on behavioral styles, you recall that Amiables and Analytics tend to move more slowly than Expressives and Drivers. That generally shows up, also, in their speed of speaking and in some of the other voice qualities (such as pitch and volume). To identify a person's personal and habitual vocal qualities, listen for individual characteristics in the following areas:

    a. General *sound* of the voice.

        1) How *resonant* is the voice? Some voices have high or full resonance in which the voice carries many minute vibrations which lend richness to it and make it sound like it comes from a full use of vocal and nasal chambers.

        2) What is the characteristic *pitch?* This refers to the highness or lowness of the sounds produced. It results from the degree of tightening or relaxing the vocal cords; however, some people characteristically speak at a higher, tighter level — a higher pitch — than others.

3) What is the characteristic *volume* of the person's natural speaking voice? This refers to how loudly the person speaks. Some people habitually speak very softly, others very loudly, others at a moderate level.

b. *Movement* of the sounds.

1) What are the *rhythmical characteristics* of the voice? Can you pick out how the sound patterns repeat across sentences? Some voices seem to flow, rising and falling in waves. Some voices rise near the middle of sentences, or at the ends, or at the beginnings. Some voices seem to keep an even beat, while others repeatedly speed up and then drop in speed.

2) What is the *general speed* of the voice? Does the person characteristically speak rapidly? Slowly?

c. *Clarity* of the sounds.

Does the person generally enunciate well or poorly? Can you hear each syllable? Are sounds like "D" and "T" always clear?

2. **Note changes from the characteristic vocal qualities,** both as to kind and direction of change.

Once you know a person's characteristic vocal qualities, you can be alert for these. When people change from their normal vocal habits, watch out; they are communicating something extra. It may indicate a point of emphasis, of importance, of concern, or of a shift in thinking or attention. Catch these hints at an early stage, and you can often do something about the direction of the communication.

So, how do you tell by these rather subtle cues whether the trend is in a positive or negative direction? First, remember this is a *refinement* of skills; it takes time to learn. You can grow into skillful use of the techniques over time, and your selling world won't end before you gain a high level of skill. Now let's look at what some of the changes can mean to you.

Upward Changes in Volume and Speed:

Generally, this indicates a change in a positive direction. Joy, cheer, and enthusiasm all emerge from this kind of change. But so does anger. If the rhythm is clipped (from what is a normal flow), probe very sensitively to clear up the communication and eliminate a potential growth in anger. If the rhythm is not clipped, you may still want to verify the implication of the change.

Downward Changes in Volume and Speed:

Generally, this tendency raises a warning. Some of the emotions to which this change is a prelude are boredom, sadness, and affection (misplaced in a sales environment). However, it could indicate satisfaction, especially if the pitch rises. So, note the change and check it out. Hints on how to check out change follow this section.

Greater Resonance and Lessened Clarity:

These characteristics generally go along with downward changes in volume and speed, and also raise a flag, a warning. Once again, however, they could indicate a movement toward satisfaction. Picking this out is important as part of your decision to move on to another stage of the sale or in circumventing negative characteristics.

Changes in Rhythm:

As in music, when something is about to happen, when there is to be a change in mood, the rhythm changes. So it is in vocal patterns. What these changes indicate varies greatly in the individual situations. But be alert to any changes and check them out. Move more carefully when the rhythm becomes clipped, as this is characteristic of anger and defensiveness. Take care, also, with a more drawn out rhythm. The person may only be pondering a point, or he or she may be expressing disbelief.

Remember that ANY change may be the client's application of conscious change in order to stress a point, to be sure you understand something of importance. Your responsibility, then, is to fall back on your listening and probing skills to get at the root of the change.

Once your listening and probing skills have determined the positive or negative nature of the change, you can do something about the situation. Often, the very act of sensitive probing will turn a negative situation around. Here, be sure to listen for changes back to the characteristic vocal qualities. You can encourage favorable trends by increased signs of interest and support or, where appropriate, by moving on in the sales process. When you probe, remember that although you may be hearing changes in vocal characteristics, what you are hearing said is the meaning of the words. Speak to the client (where you bring it up) in terms of how the *message* is coming across to you, not in terms of the vocal qualities noted.

Using Vocal Qualities for Better Communication

Even as you get information from your client by listening to the vocal qualities, so your client gets information from you. Certain characteristics of these qualities seem to help convey a sense of competence. Try to work on developing these.

1. Develop a voice that is easy to listen to. This implies the following characteristics:

   a. Strong, full resonance that doesn't overwhelm.

   b. Relaxed pitch.

   c. Controlled volume that fills, but does not extend beyond, the speaking space.

2. Enunciate clearly. Your words are important. Convey this by taking care to speak them distinctly. This will also help your client listen to them more easily. Speak each syllable clearly and concentrate on pronouncing your endings to words.

3. Use changes to emphasize points.

   a. Lower the speed at important points.

   b. Pause slightly after important points to let the message settle.

   c. Raise or lower the volume. Either will emphasize the point stated. Raised volume will tend to indicate optimism and enthusiasm. Lowered volume tends to sound confidential and concerned.

4. Provide variety in the rhythm, pitch, and volume. A monotone or obviously patterned rhythm is boring to the listener. It creates a distraction, a "noise."

5. Finally, though this is not a vocal quality, watch your client. Emphasize the points that appear of interest by using the techniques mentioned above. As you can see, timing in speaking and using vocal qualities is helpful to you and informative to your client.

A study at Yale University revealed that the poorer use of vocal qualities a person had while speaking with a client, the greater the speaker's discomfort and anxiety. Thus, good use of vocal qualities ties in with the whole concept of trust and confidence: tension up, trust down; tension down, trust (and sales) up.

7

Image: The Silent Persuader

"FIRST IMPRESSIONS are lasting impressions." At least they are strong enough to make serious salespeople work at creating an effective initial image. A good first impression sets up the chance for an easy flow of communication.

The first impression on a prospective client is the total visual image projected. It is the combined effect of many things; among them your mode of dress, your grooming, the accessories you carry, even how you choose to stand or sit. If you start off well, you move more easily into vocal and verbal communication where you will get to show your knowledge and competence and use behavioral flexibility techniques. If you fail to make a good first impression, you will have to work exceptionally hard with these other skills to improve the impression — if you can. Your client may decide whether or not to do business or even listen to you based on this first impression of you, regardless of the merits of yourself, your product, or your company.

Behind the messages in this chapter are two facts of human nature. The first is that people do indeed judge a book by its cover, despite the irrationality of the act. It is the rare person who can overcome the liability of a bad initial impression so as to realize the benefits of the genuine skills hidden underneath. Therefore, a wise action is to take care only to reveal the most flattering hints about oneself. Second, people react in a generally predictable manner to certain qualities of the "cover," the image. That may be equally irrational, but salespeople who attend to the guidelines of dress and grooming tend to sell better. Perhaps it is because the client is more comfortable in dealing with an element of predictability. When so much is unpredictable and new, as in developing a client-seller relationship, the seller owes the client as much help as possible in the endeavor — and the buyer rewards this by being initially more responsive in the sales situation.

So how does one produce a positive image, both initially, and then to sustain and forward the selling relationship? That is what the rest of this and the following chapters are about. This chapter stresses how you can enhance the way you communicate visually through projecting an appropriate image.

Dress as a Statement

Research has shown that you can change reactions to yourself by changing some aspect of your style of dress. This makes the "art" of dressing a powerful tool in any interpersonal situation. Clothes may not make the person, but they make a lasting statement about who the person is.

No matter what a person does for a living, he chooses a uniform which is really an extension of himself — a visible statement of his personality. An individual has a wide range of styles, within boundaries set by society, from which to dress to inform those around him about his personality. It, therefore, becomes important to understand what you reveal by how you dress.

People tend to dress either to gain acceptance by some social group or, in rare instances, to declare they are not part of a group. Go to any country club, tennis club, or yacht club and notice the similarity of dress styles. Look at the dress of many "radicals" and see how different the dress is from the group rebelled against — and how similar radicals of like persuasion dress. Watch women's and, more recently, men's fashion changes and notice how fast people adopt them. They are conforming to a group norm. In some large firms dress codes, written or unwritten, dictate what is acceptable. One firm comes to mind where all salespeople had to wear dark, solid-color suits; white shirts; narrow, dark ties; and traditional wingtip shoes. When women were hired, a similar "uniform" was prescribed. The firm's management felt the salespeople related better to customers that way.

Since clothing is such an important part of acceptance in human interactions, extra care is needed in maintaining an appearance that is appropriate for the type of clients to be met. This section is specifically on dressing for business acceptance and success.

Guidelines for Dressing for Sales Success

Clothing is a powerful image-maker. Research suggests that you can take two people, dress them identically, except for one detail. It could be the width of stripe in the suit, the color of the fabric, the pattern in the tie or scarf, or the color and shape of the briefcase. Just change one detail, and people will predictably pick one of the two as more successful. Since clients like to be associated with success and since they are uncomfortable with the unexpected types of dress where salespeople are concerned, the following guidelines can become powerful contributors to your sales relations — and your actual success.

1. Where possible, dress in a conservative mode. This is true for both men and women. For men, the most accepted business uniform has been and still is the simple, single-breasted suit, with or without a vest. Traditional leather wingtips and other tie shoes are recommended. Although the idea of conservative clothing remains, the expression of it can vary with the territory, as is evidenced by the difference in the city salesperson and the booted and jeaned rural seller of farm equipment.

2. Use conservative colors and patterns as well as styles.

    The conservative approach tends to give you a stability that a faddish or extreme style cannot capture. Solid colors are the most widely accepted for business suits. Some extremely subtle and conservative plaids and pinstripes are also acceptable. Effective colors for business suits are all ranges of gray, blue, and beige. As a general rule, the darker color the suit, the greater the air of authority. Shirt or blouse colors should complement the suit, not detract from the overall look or call undue attention to it.

3. If you are not sure of the circumstances of a selling situation, dress more — rather than less — conservatively than normal.

4. Assure a good fit in your clothing. Every effort should be taken to ensure proper fit whether the suit is custom-made or purchased "off the rack." Proper styling and fit are imperative to an overall neat and well-put-together appearance.

5. Dress simply. Present a clean, uncluttered appearance. To do this, follow the rules of conservative dress and extend the concept of simplicity to the accessories you wear or carry.

6. Natural fibers in clothing or accessories tend to project a success image and lend an air of authority. They include wool suits, cotton shirts, silk blouses, and silk ties. Leather, also, is better than plastic products for shoes, belts, and briefcases.

7. Dress as well as the people to whom you are selling. This allows the client to feel easier associating with you. It removes one more potential communication barrier.

Putting It All Together

The major component of your wardrobe is your suit. Everything else — shoes, shirts, blouses, ties, scarves, socks, and accessories — complements it. The positive effect of your "physical image" can be lost if the above suggestions are followed with no thought to the total image created when all elements of your dress are put together. What is the first image that comes to your mind when you see someone wearing a light suit, a darker shirt, and a light tie? How about when you see someone wearing a plaid suit, a striped shirt, and a patterned tie? Following all of the above dress suggestions is not enough. They must be combined effectively to project an overall appropriate image.

The colors you wear should be complementary to each other. For instance, your belt and shoes should match; your tie or scarf should pick up some of the color in your suit and some of the color in your shirt or blouse, if it is other than white; and your socks should blend with your suit and/or shoes. Wearing a long-sleeve shirt or blouse with a suit polishes the overall dress image even further.

Grooming for Sales Success

As with dress, simplicity and good sense guide the grooming of an image-aware salesperson. Keep hair neat and clean. Men should have a conservative, recently trimmed cut. Avoid putting anything on the hair that makes it look shiny and greasy. Women's hair is best shoulder length, which is also easy to keep up. Guidelines to the application of makeup also center on moderation. A clean, natural look is preferable. Avoid heavy makeup and perfumes.

Always be clean; it is not always necessary to be obsessively neat, but it is imperative to be clean. Check yourself in the mirror whenever possible.

Accessories and the Sales Image

Several guidelines on the wearing and carrying of accessories grow out of etiquette and common sense.

1. Avoid all but the simplest jewelry, and wear it in moderation.

2. Avoid any item that identifies any personal association or belief, unless you are absolutely sure that the person to whom you are selling shares these beliefs.

3. When used, make sure the accessories are of good quality. Fine pen and pencil sets and top quality leather attache cases speak quietly of success and pride in one's profession.

4. Never wear sunglasses or glasses that change tint as the light changes. People must see your eyes if they're to believe you.

Image Opportunities

When entering a client's place of business, you want to be taken seriously. If you appear to have authority and influence, you will be admitted more often and more quickly. Once in the presence of a client, your message will be taken more seriously if you look like you have the authority to back up your words. Therefore, it is necessary for you to exude confidence, success, and experience.

Physical characteristics can either help or hinder in this process. The tall person has a natural edge because size alone lends greater authority. However, this large size can work against a person who becomes so overpowering as to unnerve a prospective buyer. The smaller person may have the opposite problem. Charm may come across more easily; but without a sizable authoritative air to overcome the lack of size, the small person's ideas also may be seen as "small" and not taken seriously.

Clothes may alleviate both of these problems by emphasizing or de-emphasizing power. For instance, the tall person could wear soft colors and textures and avoid dark, heavy, overpowering clothing such as severely tailored suits, pinstripes, or wingtip shoes. On the other hand, the small person may find it helpful to wear high-power clothing, such as dark, pinstriped suits, vests, solid white shirts and wingtip shoes for men; or darkly colored, rich, severely tailored suits with a plain, high-quality blouse for women.

The relationship of the age of the seller to the age of the buyer can also affect the normal process of the sale. A youthful salesperson selling to an older client has essentially the same problems as the smaller person. The older salesperson selling to a young client would seem to have it made. However, since age carries its own authority, care must be taken not to come across too strongly. A young buyer may feel intimidated if an older salesperson appears too authoritative. Again, dress can help remedy these sales problems, this time associated with age. The young salesperson should generally wear high-power, conservative suits when selling to his elders. The older salesperson doesn't need to emphasize authority. Less high-powered suits and accessories are appropriate for an encounter with a younger client, so long as the salesperson doesn't understress. Keep to the general guidelines.

Geography also plays an important part in determining the successful salesperson's style of dress. Unwritten rules guide dress in each part of the country. Violating these unwritten norms can be embarrassing. This is especially important in selling because you want to make the client feel comfortable with you so that a lasting trust bond can develop. If you wear something that conspicuously labels you as different, this lack of congruence can lead to confusion and suspicion on the part of the buyer and ultimately to a lost sale. For example, if you come from a sophisticated part of the country, be sure to leave your Ivy League apparel at home when you're visiting the average rural community. The other extreme is also to be avoided. The smart small town salesperson traveling to a city dresses to fit in with the more sophisticated businessmen of the large cities.

Be careful not to endanger a sales relationship by overdressing. Your suit may be as luxurious as good taste and income allow when you're dealing with people who can afford to dress well, but be careful not to give the impression of looking down on those of a lower socioeconomic background.

By altering the color and style of your suits, you can modify your image to appeal more to buyers of all classes, to come across with higher or lower authority, or to overcome natural height and weight image problems.

Your clothes, your grooming, and the accessories you wear and carry do make a significant difference in the reception you receive from your clients because, throughout the initial phases of the sales process, first impressions do count — and if you do not present an appropriate image to create a positive impression on your clients, those first impressions will count against you.

8

Selling Without Words: The Language of Nonverbal Communication

"He that has eyes to see and ears to hear may convince himself that no mortal may keep a secret. If his lips are silent, he chatters with his fingertips; betrayal oozes out of him at every pore." Sigmund Freud

AS THE opening quote emphasizes, people tell volumes about what they think or feel even when they remain silent. This is their body language, those physical gestures and positionings which reveal thoughts and attitudes. Body language, like image, is communicated visually. It involves movements or positions from the most subtle raising of an eyebrow, to the precise movements of the trained public speaker, to the obvious leaning forward of an interested listener.

Some body language involves universal symbolism. Raising the hands over the head has long symbolized surrender and submission. Taking position at the head of the table indicates leadership.

Body language can be even more expressive than words. Conjure up the image of a person slapping his forehead. This may be accompanied by an audible groan. Don't you know already the person has just remembered something he should have done? Implicit in the gesture is also an apology to the audience for the slight.

Think, too, of the well-known gestures of saluting, tipping one's hat, shaking hands, shrugging the shoulders, waving goodbye, forming a round "O" with the thumb and forefinger, and blowing a kiss. All are forms of body language. All communicate something to those around.

Body language communication is rapid. Research shows that even when exposure to a situation is reduced to 1/24 of a second (the time it takes to show a single frame of film), people often grasp the meaning. At 3/24 of a second, comprehension goes up dramatically and rises somewhat more up to a little beyond one second. Therefore, a body position or gesture that lasts just over one second will generally be understood by a person sensitive to body language.

Ability to understand body language is apparently not related to IQ, ability to take tests, or other signs of academic achievement. Practice is the only thing that tends to improve how well people understand its messages. People who were tested for body language comprehension generally scored higher on second and succeeding tests.

Reading body language gives you a powerful communication tool. Through body language, people express their conscious and subconscious emotions, desires, and attitudes. As body language is stimulated by a subconscious need to express feelings, it is often more reliable than verbal communication. It may even contradict the verbal expressions. Thus, body language, as an outlet for feelings, can function as a lie detector to aid a watchful listener in interpreting words. If you are observant, you can read in body language a client's current level of sincerity and commitment and have an additional tool for testing the progress of the sales relationship and perhaps moving that relationship in a more positive, trust-building direction.

In addition to increasing your understanding of your client, the study of body language can also help improve the client's understanding of you. Body language is an important part of having your client perceive the sales message the way you wish it to be perceived. The better able you are to transmit your message so that your client receives it as you intended, the more effective your sales presentation will be.

This chapter explores three major areas of skill in dealing with and using body language. They are time-tested and presented to give you an overview of this extensively studied kind of communication. First, we discuss the implications of individual, often-observed gestures. These, however, are insufficient communications unless worked at in the second way — as clusters of gestures which together state a message. Finally, we look at proxemics, the communication given by the placement and proximity of two or more people. Here are clues to using physical space wisely, with sensitivity to the needs of the other person.

Interpreting Body Language Gestures

Body language involves the interpretation of many kinds of body gestures. Major areas of the body which communicate are the face (especially the eyes and lips), hands, arms, legs, body posture, and walk. Following are some of the more simple gestures that, once learned, will aid you in interpreting the feelings and attitudes that your client may not communicate to you verbally but will reveal through body language.

The Face

The face is one of the most reliable indicators of a person's attitude and feelings. You know that we have the word "poker face" for anyone who is striving to hide a feeling by means of keeping a guarded expression. The face is such a good indicator that professional poker players practice maintaining the same facial expression throughout a game to prevent giving the opposition a clue as to the quality of the cards being held.

Eyes

Think of the terms "shifty eyes," "beady eyes," "a look of steel," or "windows of the soul." All refer to eyes and are just a sampling of the awareness people have for the communications coming from the eyes. The comfortable person has a tendency to look you straight in the eyes when speaking. Clients tend to avoid eye contact with you when an uncomfortable question is asked. Therefore, monitor eye contact during your conversations and pursue topics that increase it. They build trust. If you can, steer clear of topics that decrease eye contact, for they increase tension and reduce trust. We talk about increase and decrease of eye contact, for people have habitual tendencies and the cue lies in a movement away from the habitual contact, not in some definable amount of contact.

People tend to have more eye contact when they listen than when they talk. A client's eye contact with you usually indicates interest in what you are saying or doing.

Smiles

Smiles usually indicate approval and enjoyment. However, two kinds of smiles have been noted as danger signals to meaningful communication. The "simple smile" is a slight turning up of the corners of the lips without exposing any teeth. This indicates a probable lack of interest and a mind preoccupied with things other than the ongoing conversation. In the "oblong smile," the lips are drawn fully back from both the upper and lower teeth, forming an oblong shape. The smile appears to lack depth or real involvement in any of the ongoing feelings. The client is probably unappreciative of the remarks or activity. Generally, unlike the simple smile, some eye contact exists.

Hands to Face or Head

When a client rubs a portion of his face or head, he is perhaps signaling doubt, disinterest, or frustration. If the finger rubs near the eye or the ear, doubt or lack of interest is likely. Frustration is often indicated when the hand or palm rubs the back of the head or neck ("You're a pain in the neck?") and may be identified at an early stage when the client starts running a finger along the inside of a shirt or blouse collar.

Rubbing or touching the nose usually indicates a strong feeling of dislike. It is almost as much of a NO signal as when the client uses the word. While people will rub their nose because it itches, keep in mind there is a difference in mannerism. The gesture in question here is a light rubbing, subtle and often accompanied with

98

squirming in the chair, twisting the body into a silhouette position, physically withdrawing.

Distinguish rubbing from the thoughtful stroking of the fingers on the chin. This indicates consideration, careful study, and analysis. The client may not be convinced of your stand, but is not tuning you out. A congruent facial expression with this gesture is a slight squinting of the eyes, as if trying to see an answer to the problem in the distance.

Pinching the bridge of the nose, when accompanied with closed eyes, usually communicates great thought and concern about the information you are presenting. A client who is in great conflict with what he is hearing may well lower his head and pinch the bridge of the nose to see if he is in such a predicament or only having a "bad dream."

Other hand-to-face motions that telegraph messages to the alert listener follow. For ease of presentation, they are in list form.

1. Leaning back with both hands supporting the head may well show a feeling of superiority.

2. Hands to the mouth is often a gesture of astonishment, but it's also seen after a member of the group has raised a question. This usually indicates the individual is sorry or surprised at the question or comment.

3. When both hands are cupped over the mouth, the client may be trying to hide an attitude or is only waiting for a chance to inject a negative comment or idea into the conversation.

4. Tugging at the ear may well indicate the client wants to interrupt.

5. Boredom is often telegraphed when a client rests his head in his open palm, drops his chin in a nodding manner, and allows his eyelids to droop.

6. Hand to cheek, fingers bent, and index finger to temple usually indicates an interest and attentiveness, especially when associated with your client leaning forward in the chair (or leaning forward from a standing position) toward you.

7. A similar pose that expresses a critical evaluation is the forefinger placed near the nose with the chin resting in the palm and fingers bent across the chin and below the mouth. When this is associated with the body drawn back and positioned away from you, the thoughts are usually critical, cynical, or in some other way negative toward what you are doing or saying.

Hand to Hand

1. Tightly clenched hands usually indicate the client is being over-powered and suspects you of trying to impose an attitude. Tightly clasped hands with stares, a side-turned body, and crossed legs indicate that you have gone too far. The clenched hand conveys strong disagreement. The client will usually be tense and difficult to relate to.

2. Wringing hands is a stepped-up version of the clenched hands gesture. This may well indicate the client feels placed on the "hot seat."

3. Rubbing of the palms is usually indicative of a feeling of expectation. This is not to be confused with wringing the hands. This is a soft rubbing gesture by which the client conveys interest and involved anticipation of what you are going to say or do.

4. Steepling (joining the fingertips together and forming what might be described as a church steeple): indicates a smugness in a client who is sure of his or her stand and is expressing great self-confidence.

5. Low steepling: This is the same gesture as No. 4 above, but done much lower, at the waist or on the lap. This lower steepling gesture may indicate a lesser degree of the same self-confidence. Women seem to show this more than men.

6. High steepling: Usually done around the face, this indicates smugness and self-confidence. Often, the client looks at you through the fingers, which may indicate a feeling of superiority.

7. Subtle steepling: When one hand is placed upon the other in a modified steepling gesture, it may well indicate a cautious client, only somewhat confident.

8. Tight steepling: This is when the hands are joined more closely and the arms assume the basic position of other steepling gestures. This frequently indicates confidence.

9. Hands joined together at the back: Though this is not very comfortable when sitting, it is sometimes done and indicates authority. This is especially seen when a client is standing and generally indicates a superior attitude.

Crossed Arms

Crossed arms tend to signal defensiveness. They seemingly act as a protective guard against an anticipated attack or a fixed position from which the client would rather not move. As long as your client is in this position, it is unlikely you will get full agreement to what you are saying or doing.

Crossed Legs

Crossed legs tend to signal disagreement. Clients who tightly cross their legs seem to be telling you they disagree with what you are saying or doing. Crossed legs and crossed arms usually indicate extreme negativeness to what is going on.

Sitting

1. Sitting with the chair back facing forward and straddling the seat, with arms on the chairback, tends to express a superior attitude, dominance, and aggression.

2. Sitting on the edge of the chair, leaning forward, usually indicates interest and involvement.

3. Sitting facing a door (or standing facing a door) usually means the client is ready to leave or have you leave and is waiting for an opportunity.

4. Sitting with a leg over the arm of a chair can signal an uncooperative individual. Often the client is unconcerned about or hostile to the situation.

5. Sitting taut and erect, feet flat on the floor, staring with unblinking eyes may mean a client is not paying attention; his or her mind is far away. It is often an attempt to look interested without being involved.

6. Sitting with legs crossed and the elevated foot moving in a slight kicking motion usually indicates boredom or impatience.

Handling Accessories

The way a client handles accessories also communicates. To give you an idea (only) of the enormous breadth involved in reading gestures involving accessories, we present only one — that of handling eyeglasses. The scope and aims of this book curtail our going into the encyclopedic list of meanings inherent in a full exploration of gestures with accessories. However, many (not all) of the gestures involved with eyeglasses extend to other accessories and things within reach, such as pens and pencils.

1. Dropping the glasses onto the lower bridge of the nose and peering over them often indicates disbelief.

2. A client who slowly and deliberately removes glasses and carefully cleans them is involved in deep thought. When repeated, it may indicate a stalling for time and a desire to think over your proposal at some future time. It may also indicate a desire to pose a question, ask for clarification, or raise opposition. Be prepared to probe for the reason.

3. A similar gesture to gain time is one in which the glasses are removed and the earpiece is put in the mouth. This may well indicate the client is trying to keep from speaking in order to listen more intently. It may also telegraph a craving for more information.

4. Occasionally, you may see a client quickly and with much emphasis remove his or her glasses and toss them onto the table, his or her lap, or the floor (if he or she is sitting without a table nearby). This gesture usually indicates you have gone too far in your line of reasoning. In such cases, the client is com-

municating resistance to what is being said. A clarifying probe may help here. ("Do you see how...?")

5. With glasses in hand, held by the earpiece, lenses dangling downward, and the same hand resting against the face, the client is probably tuning you out and is ready to leave. This is especially true when the torso is turned slightly away from you. This brings us to gesture clusters. These are the series of gestures which together provide clues to how your client is receiving you and your message.

Interpreting and Using Gesture Clusters

Be sure to base analysis of your client's body language on a series of signals to be sure that the message is coming across in several ways and is not misinterpreted through misreading an isolated gesture. A single gesture may be meaningless. When gestures are interpreted in clusters, however, the combined result is a rather clear message.

Certain combinations of gestures are especially reliable indicators of people's feelings. They may be used to augment, emphasize, contradict, or be unrelated to verbal pronouncements. Therefore, reading body language messages through interpreting gesture clusters is a continuous process of analysis. Major gesture clusters that convey meaning are presented on the following pages.

Openness

In this situation, your client signals sincerity and a cooperative attitude, as he wants to work toward an agreeable solution with you. This attitude is characterized by:

1. Open hands.
2. Unbuttoned coat collar.
3. Taking coat off.
4. Getting together by moving closer.
5. Leaning forward in chair.
6. Uncrossed legs.
7. Arms gently and loosely crossing lower body.

Enthusiasm

1. Small upper or inward smile.
2. Erect body stance.
3. Hands open, arms extended.
4. Eyes wide and alert.
5. Lively and bouncy.
6. Voice lively and well modulated.

Defensiveness

When your client feels in psychological danger, he assumes a defensive position. This position is characterized by:

1. Rigid body.
2. Arms or legs crossed tightly in protective gestures.
3. Minimal eye contact with occasional sideways or darting glances.
4. Pursed lips.
5. Head down with chin depressed toward the chest.
6. Fists clenched.
7. Fingers clenching the crossed arms.
8. Leaning back in chair.

Anger

Assuming that self-control is maintained, the anger body gestures are:

1. Body rigid.
2. Fists clenched.
3. Lips closed and held in a tight thin line.
4. Continued eye contact with dilation of pupils.
5. Sometimes squinting of eyes.
6. Shallow breathing.

In a sales situation, the defensive gesture cluster means little chance of a sale unless you can effect an attitude change in your client. You must change your approach. Probe to get at the place where your communication has broken down.

Two other postures which indicate a defensive attitude are body positions with the leg over the arm of a chair, or straddling a chair. Each warns of hostility or a domineering attitude.

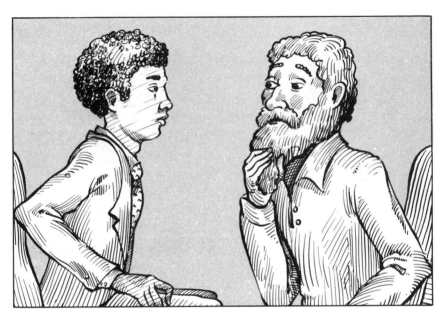

Readiness

This positive situation is characterized by:

1. Leaning forward in a chair in an open position.
2. Hand possibly placed midthigh.
3. Relaxed, but alive, facial expression.
4. Standing with hands on hips; feet slightly spread.

Evaluation

When your client is listening intently to your words in order to judge their merit, the body position shows evaluative gestures. These include:

1. Sitting in the front portion of the chair with the upper torso projected forward.
2. Slightly tilted head.
3. Hand to cheek gesture, where head is often supported by the hand.
4. Stroking of the chin or pulling the beard.

Nervousness

Common indicators of nervousness are:

1. Clearing throat.
2. Hand-to-mouth movements.
3. Covering the mouth when speaking.
4. Tugging at ear.
5. Darting eyes or failure to maintain eye contact.
6. Twitching lips or face.
7. Mouth just slightly open.
8. Playing with objects and fidgeting.
9. Shifting weight while standing.
10. Tapping fingers.
11. Waving foot in a circular motion.
12. Plucking at collar or ringing neck with finger inside shirt collar.
13. Incongruent laugh.
14. Pacing.
15. Whistling.
16. Tugging at clothes.
17. Jingling money in pockets.

Critical Evaluation

In this situation, which is generally less desirable than the evaluation gesture cluster, your client will:

1. Be more drawn back.
2. Have hand to cheek, or chin in palm, with all fingers under the mouth except the index finger, which follows the side of the nose.

Suspicion and Secrecy

These attitudes can be recognized by such gestures as:

1. Failing to make eye contact or resisting glances from you.
2. Glancing sideways at you by slightly turning the body away.
3. Rubbing or touching the nose.
4. Squinting or peering over glasses.

The first sign of suspicion and secrecy may be an unrelated and incongruent pattern of gestures. There may be a conflict between what your client says and what his or her body projects, or there may be a series of incongruent body gestures. In these cases, expect secrecy.

Rejection and Doubt

Rejection and doubt are characterized by some of the same gestures as suspicion and secrecy, as they all are related feelings which indicate a negative reaction. These include:

1. Touching and rubbing nose.
2. Squinting eyes or rubbing eyes.
3. Arms and legs crossed.
4. Body withdrawn.
5. Throat clearing.
6. Hand rubbing or ear tugging.
7. Glancing sideways.
8. Raising an eyebrow.

Confidence and Authority

Easily recognized gestures include:

1. Steepling (the higher the hands held, the greater the confidence).
2. Resting feet on the desk.
3. Leaning back with hands laced behind head.
4. Holding hands together behind back with chin thrust forward.
5. Proud, erect body stance with shoulders squared.
6. Continuing eye contact with little blinking.
7. Smiling inwardly.
8. Reducing hand-to-face gestures.
9. Tipping back in chair.

Reassurance

In order to reassure themselves, clients may:

1. Pinch the fleshy part of their hands.
2. Gently rub or caress some personal object such as a ring, watch, or necklace.
3. Bite fingernails or examine cuticles.

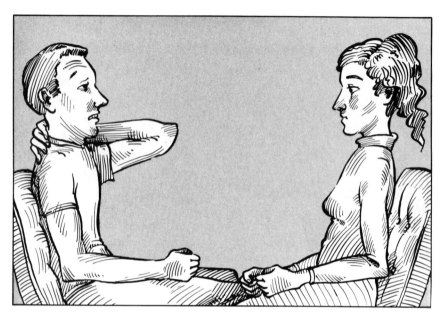

Frustration

Clients exhibit frustration through the following gestures:

1. Tightly clenched hands or shaking fists.
2. Hand wringing.
3. Rubbing back of neck.
4. Controlled, short breathing.
5. Blind staring.
6. Running hands through hair.
7. Tightly closed lips.
8. Stamping a foot.
9. Pacing.

Self-Control

Self-control gestures are manifested when your client is holding something back. They include:

1. Wrists gripped behind the back.
2. Crossed and locked ankles.
3. Fists clenched.
4. Pupils contracted.
5. Lips closed or pursed.

Boredom and Indifference

If you see these gestures, check for boredom or indifference:

1. Head in hand.
2. Drooping eyelids.
3. Relaxed posture; slouching.
4. Tapping of foot or fingers.
5. Swinging of feet.
6. Blank stares, little eye contact.
7. Doodling.
8. Slack lips.
9. Posture aimed at exit.

Acceptance

A client shows acceptance by displaying honesty and sincerity. This includes:

1. Spreading hands held to chest (for men).
2. Moving closer to the other person.

Give special considerations to the conditions that exist during a sales presentation which provide opportunities for you to effectively use body language. It can be an ally to reduce tensions and move the sales relationship in a positive direction.

Basically, be aware of the nonverbal cues which people constantly emit. Inconsistency in gestures indicates secrecy, but this secrecy can be working to your advantage. A client sits in her office, stating firmly that she's not yet ready to purchase your product since the one she currently has is adequate. At the same time, she taps her feet or drums her fingers on the desk, while her stern face and tone of voice indicate that she is not buying. According to several studies, the uneasy gestures betray that she is really seriously considering your product.

Another positive sign that a client is moving toward a purchase is *an upward look with rapid blinking*. Chances are, whatever you have been discussing is being seriously considered. The client may have already made a favorable decision on the big issue and may be meditating on the details. Patience is needed here. Refrain from further sales talk until the meditation is complete.

Look for changes in body postures and gestures. They often indicate a comparable change in mental attitudes. If a client decides to buy, the most obvious signs are *relaxation* — unlocking of ankles, palms extended outwardly toward you; movement toward the front of the chair generally accompanies this. All indicate the client is listening, tuning in, ready to move ahead. The client may start to *nod* in agreement and even *copy* your gestures. Recognize these signs and move to the next stage of the sales process. Otherwise, you may start to oversell and risk boring the client. Even if you have a list of benefits yet to convey, resist. As long as your basic commitments to the client in the sales process have been fulfilled, move on; move at the client's speed.

Changes, of course, may be in a negative direction also. Be wary of the change in which the client tightens up, closes his or her limbs, leans back. You are probably not being effective. The client is not showing receptivity. Alter your approach when this happens.

Be as aware of your own body positions as you are of those of your client. You, too, send signals. Even if your client is not trained in reading the more subtle of them, he or she will still be affected by what you project. For instance, if you greet your client with a slap on the back (assuming this is strictly a business acquaintance), the client may feel uneasy without being able really to express why. In North America, a firm, warm handshake is the only accepted and helpful form of contact with a client. Other forms of touching are reserved for close associates and friends. Again, if during your sales discussion you look comfortably straight eye-to-eye (prop your glasses on your head if you wear them), your client will get a positive feeling even if the reason for this is obscure.

As a matter of fact, your gesture clusters can directly affect the gestures of your client. Studies have demonstrated that people who exhibit "expressionless stimuli" such as blank expressions and a removed, disinterested air produce lowered amounts of expression in others. A simple head nod in agreement encourages the same in your client, while a combination of head nods and warm smiles seems to open the client to expressing similar feelings when used with restraint. People who sit in open, relaxed positions are seen as more persuasive, active, and better liked than those who sit in a tight, closed manner. These more open people are also able to effect greater opinion change than those who are closed. On the other hand, defensiveness, anger, or frustration on the part of your clients may be a direct result of aggressiveness, dominance, or other negative body language on your part.

Both the reading and the projecting of body language clusters are important in a sales relationship. One influence which we have not yet talked about is that of the distance and direction of the movement. Proxemics deals with that.

Proxemics

Proxemics involves the study of space and the movement of people within it. In other words, it talks about where you stand (sit) and how you move around within your space to ease and aid communication. Haven't you had someone stand so close that you felt you could analyze what that person had for lunch? If so, weren't you uncomfortable? How do you feel when someone takes your favorite cup to drink from (or uses a favorite item — your special pencil, perhaps)? That uncomfortable feeling results from a proxemic violation. Proxemics is another influence on the communication process. In fact, it is a specific and recognizable form of nonverbal communication.

Proxemic Zones

Humans tend to keep distances, or zones, between themselves and others. These zones, "bubbles" of space, around a person are actually extensions of that person's behavioral style. Another influence on the dimensions of proxemic zones is culture. Our discussion will assume a North American culture and will be generally applied to all behavioral styles. Figure 8-A shows the four basic zones of interaction for Americans. A sales relationship generally begins in the "social zone" of 4 to 12 feet. Closer than four feet, only at the client's invitation, the salesperson moves into the personal space. Outside of the initial handshake, a sales relationship does not intrude into the intimate zone unless the client is a back-slapping Expressive or an Amiable with an occasional need to touch. This is done at the *client's* invitation, and only after a professional relationship has been well established.

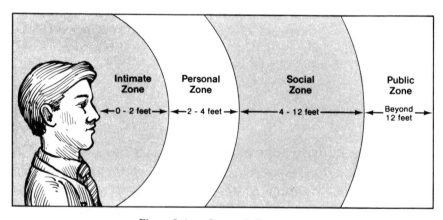

Figure 8-A   Proxemic Zones

People are not always conscious of the importance of maintaining these distances. When you commit a proxemic violation with your client, he or she generally has only a feeling that something is wrong. The cause may not be identified. It would be better if the cause were noted, for then, at least, the client would know the source of uneasiness and not tend to blame your product or your attitude. Your client may even look inward for the cause and become self-conscious. In this situation, the client's attention shifts to the inappropriate proxemic behavior rather than the conversation at hand. Communication breakdown occurs. Positive, productive sales interaction is interrupted.

The sales implications of proxemic violations should be obvious. A violation of your client's proxemic zones without verbal or nonverbal invitation most likely will lead to greater tension and decreased trust. The buyer-seller relationship deteriorates and becomes nonproductive. However, the sales relationship can also deteriorate if your client verbally or nonverbally signals that it is all right for you to move from one proxemic zone to a closer one (no sexual connotations intended) and you "refuse" the invitation. The client may then perceive you as cold and aloof and only interested in the sale rather than him or her as a person. Therefore, a proxemic violation can be twofold: trespassing into zones without invitation or refusing an invitation to move into a closer zone.

Psychological Proxemics

Up to this point, we have only been discussing "physical" proxemics. However, there is another important dimension to the study of proxemics — the "psychological" dimension. This involves mental zones — the psychological zones of a person's mind. Your ideas and language may be formal, and be in the public zone ("How-do-you-do?"); casual, as in the social zone ("Hi!"); friendly, as in the personal zone ("How's the family, Joe?"); or intimate ("Hi, dear."), as in the intimate zone. In the "Probing" chapter, we talked about probes being appropriate at some times and inappropriate at other times. Using a personal probe or an endearing term too soon, at the wrong time, or even using it at all may tend to violate another person's "psychological" space. Try calling your supervisor "Dear." (Actually, don't try; imagine the results.) This verbal intrusion can be as destructive as a physical violation of space. That is why interrogative techniques used by brainwashers, and even by some attorneys and police officers, are so intimidating. They intrude upon and violate a person's mental space.

Proxemic Categories

People can generally be classified into two major proxemic categories — contact and noncontact. When these two major patterns of proxemic behavior meet, their interaction normally ends in a clash. The contact people unknowingly get too close physically and/or psychologically to the noncontact people, whereas the noncontact people do not get close enough, physically and/or psychologically, to the contact people.

Contact and noncontact people frequently have unpleasant perceptions of each other, based upon their proxemic behavior. The noncontact people are seen as cold, unfriendly, or impolite by the contact people. On the other hand, noncontact people perceive the contact people as overly friendly, clinging, and smothering. Interestingly enough, this concept of contact and noncontact behavior relates directly to the four behavioral styles. Analytics and Drivers tend to exhibit noncontact behavior, while Expressives and Amiables have a tendency to be contact people. This helps explain why some styles "naturally" cause tension for other styles — their proxemic behaviors are incompatible.

Proxemic Territoriality

Another facet of proxemic behavior is that of territoriality. We each develop our own "turf" — a "space" for our personal property. Have you ever become upset with someone who sat in your chair? Leaned on your desk? Picked up some object of yours without your permission? Territorial proxemics in action. In fact, studies have shown clients fail to listen to what is said if the salesperson is also handling some object that belongs to the client.

When someone invades your territory, knowingly or unknowingly, you usually feel unsettled by the intrusion and feel a degree of tension. This tension eventually leads to your suspicion and distrust of the perpetrator. Now think what goes through your client's mind when you invade his or her territory. Be careful when you reach to use your client's desk set because it is handy. It is better that you use your own.

Research into territorial proxemics has revealed two categories of territory, in addition to their zones, that people attempt to protect. These include:

1. Fixed feature territory: The unmovable boundaries, such as doors to an office and the walls of a house, are fixed features.

2. Semifixed feature territory: This includes movable objects and their arrangement, such as furniture, decor items, paintings, and knickknacks.

We all like to protect and control "our" territory, but we are not always granted that desire. For instance, you seek, and often do have, control over your fixed feature territory. The walls of your office or house keep intruders out. You can shut or lock your door to keep people out. However, there are times when others intrude into your fixed feature territory. When this happens, tension levels can skyrocket and trust levels plummet. Think how you would feel if you had your door closed and someone walked into your office or your room without knocking, and uninvited. Do you, or have you, ever stop(ped) by without an appointment to visit a client and stuck your head into his or her office — without knocking and/or uninvited? How do you think it makes that client feel about you?

Not as much control can be exercised by us over our semifixed feature territory even though we'd like to control it as much as our fixed feature territory. Watch the nonverbal behavior of your clients if you move or pick up their personal objects. Their attention shifts to the object and away from the conversation. Communication is suspended. Tension goes up. Trust goes down. The irony is that it doesn't matter if that object is breakable, unbreakable, valuable, or inexpensive. All that matters to your client is that it is one's personal semifixed feature territory and you violated it.

I can recall an uncomfortable situation in which I was searching for some information in someone else's file cabinet when that person entered the room. The person had invited me to use that file drawer, but we really had not as yet organized it. There was momentary silence and a cool, "May I help you find something?" I left my hand lightly resting on the drawer and moved it back and forth as I explained what I was after. That being explained, the situation again relaxed. Had I quickly taken my hand out of the drawer, the tone would probably have remained cool, for I would also then convey guilt. Proxemic violations visibly intrude upon any communication that is occurring.

In attempting to establish a trust bond, be careful not to offend your clients by violating their proxemic zones or territory. They value their privacy and protect their territory.

You can use the concept of proxemics to improve your trust bond with your client. The sales process can be viewed as initially meeting your client face-to-face at a social distance and slowly moving 180° to a side-by-side personal distance. Care should be exercised in not moving too fast (increasing tension) or too slow (refusing your client's invitation).

Respect, understand, and effectively utilize the concepts of proxemics. If you do, the client will feel at ease, will be able to listen better, and will feel better about you than if you violate any of the proxemic guidelines. It will greatly ease your job in building the trust bond necessary for a good sales relationship.

9

Clarifying the Sales Communication Process

HAVE YOU ever completed a task, handed in the report, maybe felt really pleased — or uncomfortable — with it, and received nothing, no remarks? Did you feel tension rise within you? Didn't you wish somebody would say something — anything? A smile would help. Even some criticism would be welcome. That feeling, if you felt it, stemmed from a desire for feedback.

Feedback is important in a sales situation also. I can remember being close to agony after five minutes with a client who sat impassively, not visibly or verbally reacting to anything I said. Oh, did I wish for feedback to help me decide what to do, where to go next, with the message. I did get it, but I had to use probing skills to receive what I needed.

When you lean forward to show interest, when you frown, when you say "Let's see if I understand...," whenever you audibly or physically signal a reaction to what someone says or does, you are using feedback. Good tension-free communication depends on it.

Feedback in the sales process is often misused and misunderstood. Salespeople have been known to frustrate clients by constant interruption to "assure" proper communication. Others have sounded like they were criticizing the client instead of reacting to the client's statements. Others have forgotten the power of body language in the feedback process and have allowed unpleasant, communication-retarding signs of boredom or dislike to feed back to the client. These problems can be overcome, and proper feedback techniques learned. Properly used, feedback simply and effectively increases the accuracy of the communication between people and does a great deal to reduce tension and build trust.

This chapter explores the feedback skills you can use to clarify the communications between you and your clients and how to read and respond to the reactions to you and your message that your client reveals.

Types of Feedback

Feedback can be either verbal, where the meanings of the words provide the information ("Remember, I need that final shipment in one month."), or nonverbal, where the meaning is carried by the sounds or actions of the person rather than in the word (Well-l-l-l). Both forms of feedback can be used by you to give feedback to clients and to get feedback from clients. For instance, you give information to clients through simple statements, through probing, through vocal qualities, and through body language. You can also get feedback from clients by asking for it through your probing skills, by reading their body language, or by listening to their vocal qualities. As you no doubt notice, feedback is simply the strategic use of all our previously discussed verbal and nonverbal communication skills for the explicit purpose of testing and validating the accuracy and effectiveness of the communication. The client's change in speed of response, for example, may mean he's willing to buy or that he's suspicious of the data. If we don't determine what it is, we can bore our client or, at worst, lose the sale — and maybe the client.

Verbal Feedback

As the name implies, verbal feedback involves probes, statements, descriptions, and other spoken comments where the meanings of the words carry the feedback message. Through verbal feedback, you typically ask for clarification of feelings or thoughts. You may also feed back viewpoints or interpretations of your own to make sure that your client's understanding of your key points are on target.

Verbal feedback is useful, also, for checking on the pace and priorities established. For instance, this probe might be helpful here: "My manager tells me that I sometimes get carried away with my enthusiasm (thoroughness) and move along too quickly (slowly). Would it be more helpful to you if I covered these topics slower (faster)?" This not only shows interest in the client's desires and needs, it also lets the client understand you a bit and feel encouraged to ask you to slow down or speed up the presentation. You could ask, "Would you like me to get right into the details of the proposal, or do you have some other questions first?" This gives the client, again, a feeling that his needs are important. It also lets you sense more about him and the priorities he has. Through the resulting feedback from the client, you can then adjust your pace and priority to meet his needs, encouraging a tension-free atmosphere of trust.

Feedback lets you explain to someone else how you are interpreting not only what they say but how it comes across to you — how you are reading the nonverbal feedback you are getting.

"Shall we explore that issue some more?" (This said upon seeing increased client interest.)

"How do you think that will work?" (This upon seeing either increased or decreased interest. It attempts to get issues into the open.)

"You look puzzled. Can I explain something a little better?"

"I like the way you explained that. It made me see that the two products are connected in both..."

Feedback helps prevent errors in understanding. The abundance of meaning for even "simple" words may prompt salespeople to assume that they understand the meaning of their client's communication when, in fact, they may have misinterpreted it. Then misunderstandings arise and breakdowns in the buyer-seller communication process, decreased trust, and lost sales follow.

Interpretation of words or phrases may vary from person to person, group to group, region to region, or society to society. Even words you usually use in everyday conversations almost inevitably have multiple meanings. According to Dr. William V. Haney, in his book *Communication and Organizational Behavior*, the 500 most commonly used words in our language have a total of more than 14,000 dictionary definitions. He goes on to give an example using the word "fast," where "fast" is cited with at least twelve different meanings. Some of the meanings are even contradictory: Fast as "rapid" vs. "tied down tightly" or as "sensitive to light" (film) vs. "insensitive to antiseptics" (bacteria).

Therefore, during the whole process of communications, use feedback. This makes certain that both you and your client are speaking the same language. For example:

1. During presentation, describe to your client the relevant aspects of the image in your mind just to make sure that you both are talking about the same thing. ("I plan to show you just how this product can answer your need for ---, ---, and ---.")

2. If the client does not feed back your message, it is wise for you to ask him or her to do so. ("What do you see or think of when I say that this service is people-oriented?")

3. Feed back your interpretation rather than the client's exact words or a simple paraphrasing of his or her words. (For a client who wants a continuous training and upgrading package: "If I hear you right, you would like to be kept informed of any changes in the system and have us train you whenever, in our opinion, the change warrants it.")

Verbal feedback statements are informational in nature as indicated. Typically, feedback statements begin with statements such as:

"Let me be sure I understand your major concerns."

"Let me see if I can summarize the key points we've discussed."

"I hear you saying..."

They typically end with questions such as:

"Did I understand you properly?"

"Was I on target with what you meant?"

"Were those your major concerns?"

This allows you to clarify understanding and meaning quickly and accurately.

Nonverbal Feedback

Remember when the word "vibes" was in vogue? "Good vibes" meant something made a person feel good. Well, both good and bad vibes are a result of nonverbal feedback. Without saying a word, people can communicate the full range of attitudes and feelings: openness, enthusiasm, confidence, nervousness, indifference, defensiveness.

The skilled salesperson uses nonverbal feedback for the same overriding goal as with verbal feedback — to continue the client-seller interaction in a positive atmosphere of trust and credibility. The sensitive, perceptive salesperson takes cues from the client's nonverbal feedback to structure the content and direction of his own message. He also sends appropriate nonverbal messages to his client to enhance and clarify his verbal statements.

You have already been introduced to ways to use nonverbal communication skills to help convey your attitudes and ideas. Your vocal qualities, your image, and even how you move and choose to stand and sit carry messages. When these messages are reactions to something another person is saying and doing, and when the other person can read them, you have given nonverbal feedback. Many of your clients will be trained in reading some of the more obvious of your nonverbal feedback statements. A very few will be trained to pick up the more subtle cues. Most will merely react to what you feed back without being aware of why they are picking up the signals you are giving them — and only if your signals are "loud and clear." However, if your nonverbal feedback is under your conscious control, and if you choose to look interested and to both encourage positive and discourage negative directions, you will begin to see just how helpful nonverbal feedback can be in clearing away communication barriers.

Using Feedback

The amount of feedback you receive and send is not as important as how you interpret and react to it. It is critically important for you to realize when you are losing your client. If you are alert, your client will give you this information through diminished interest and a lowered level of responding. With sensitivity and perception, you can react to this feedback by changing your pace or topic, by probing, or by doing whatever is needed in order to recapture the client's attention and interest. On the other hand, be sensitive to client feedback that communicates it is appropriate for you to move on in the sales process.

Feedback can be used to create a sense of trust and credibility, and can reduce client tension if used properly. A client who shows heightened interest lets you know you have uncovered something important to the client. Use a feedback probe to clarify the client's needs so that there is no misunderstanding. You can use feedback also to respond as the client speaks. Most of all, use feedback to improve your sales presentation. Through feedback, you can determine the areas on which to spend more and less time.

The proper and effective use of feedback skills maintains and enhances communication with clients. This leads to less buyer-seller tension, increased trust and credibility, and a higher probability for consummating a sale.

10

Selling Prospects the Way THEY Want To Be Sold

ALTHOUGH PROBING, listening, dressing, and acting appropriately are useful tools to help meet another's needs, they are not enough. The personal behavioral style of each client affects how he or she receives your communication. To best meet client needs, therefore, you will often have to alter actions natural to your style. You need behavioral flexibility.

Behavioral flexibility is something you do to yourself, not to others. It occurs when you step out of your own "comfort zone" — your own style preferences — to meet another's needs. It occurs each time you slow down somewhat for an Amiable or an Analytic, or when you move fast or speed up for a Driver or an Expressive, if you usually move more slowly. It occurs when a Driver or an Analytic takes time to listen to human interest or family stories from an Amiable or Expressive client.

Behavioral flexibility is independent from behavioral style, and it varies greatly within styles. No style is "naturally" more flexible than another. You can choose to be flexible with some people and inflexible with others. In addition, you can choose to be flexible with one person today and inflexible with that person tomorrow. It is an individual decision to "manage" your own style so as to meet a client's style needs and reduce the possibility of that client experiencing tension. It is much like a smoker refraining from smoking in a room of nonsmokers. It is controlling one's own behavior when it makes the other people more comfortable.

Your flexibility level with others very often determines their perceptions of you. Raise your flexibility level, and they will perceive you more positively; lower it, and they will perceive you less favorably. However, it isn't quite as simple as that.

As with any good thing, too much or too little behavioral flexibility can be negative. A salesperson with too little flexibility will more than likely be viewed by others as solely or predominantly concerned with personal needs. Because he consistently acts according to his pace and priorities, he will be seen as blunt, single-minded, rigid, and non-negotiable. On the opposite end of the flexibility scale, the highly flexible salesperson runs into two other kinds of problems. Because his pace and priority needs are constantly set aside for those of his clients, he may be viewed as unpredictable or wishy-washy by those who see him interact with different people. Also, a person operating in a behavioral style that is not his own will experience tension. Usually the tension is temporary and worth the client rapport. However, a salesperson who maintains high flexibility in all interactions may not be able to avoid stress and inefficiency. The effectively flexible salesperson compromises, giving in to the speed and interests of the client, but not totally. This highest level of flexibility is reserved for sales situations or where interaction would otherwise not go well. He relaxes from it in other encounters. This salesperson meets both personal and client needs. He negotiates relationships and shares so that everybody wins. He is seen as tactful, reasonable, and understanding. This is the image the non-manipulative salesperson strives to project to others.

The following figures (10-A through 10-D) present guidelines to use in implementing behavioral flexibility as you communicate with each of the four behavioral styles.

1. For each style, think of someone who represents that style.

2. Now, in your mind, picture yourself trying out each suggestion in the list (as in Figure 10-A) as you work with that client on the problem solving for meeting needs.

3. Repeat with a new "client" until your responses are natural and come easily.

BEHAVIORAL FLEXIBILITY WITH EXPRESSIVES

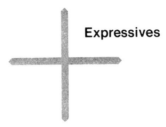

Expressives

- Get your client to talk about opinions, ideas, and dreams, and then try to support them.

- Don't hurry the discussion. Try to develop mutually stimulating ideas together.

- The Expressive does not like to lose arguments, so try not to argue. Instead, explore alternative solutions you both can share with enthusiasm.

- When you reach agreement, iron out the specific details concerning what, when, who, and how. Be sure you both agree on the specifics.

- Summarize in writing what you both agreed upon even though it may not appear necessary (don't ask permission, just do it).

- Be entertaining and fast-moving.

- Make sure you both are in full agreement concerning when actions must be performed (specification).

- The Expressive's decisions are positively affected if you use testimonials from important people or companies with which this client can identify.

Figure 10-A   Behavioral Flexibility with Expressives

BEHAVIORAL FLEXIBILITY WITH DRIVERS

Drivers

- Try to support your client's goals and objectives.

- Ask questions that allow a client to discover things rather than be told.

- Keep your relationship businesslike. Do not attempt to establish a personal relationship unless that is one of your client's objectives.

- If you disagree with a Driver, argue the facts, not personal feelings.

- Give recognition to the Driver's ideas; not to the Driver personally.

- To influence the decisions of the Driver, you should provide alternative actions with probabilities of their success (backed by facts, if available).

- Be precise, efficient, time-disciplined, and well-organized with the Driver.

Figure 10-B   Behavioral Flexibility with Drivers

BEHAVIORAL FLEXIBILITY WITH ANALYTICS

Analytics

- Try to support the Analytic's organized, thoughtful approach. Any contributions you can make toward the Analytic's objectives should be demonstrated through actions rather than words (send literature, brochures, charts, etc.).

- Be systematic, exact, organized, and prepared with the Analytic.

- List advantages and disadvantages of any plan you propose and have viable alternatives for dealing effectively with the disadvantages.

- Give the Analytic time to verify your words and actions (because the client will take the time).

- The client likes things in writing, so follow-up your personal contacts with a letter.

- Provide solid, tangible, factual evidence (not someone's opinion) that what you say is true and accurate.

- Do not rush the decision-making process.

- An Analytic likes guarantees that his or her actions can't backfire.

- Avoid gimmicks which you believe might help you in getting a fast decision (the Analytic will think something is wrong with your plan).

Figure 10-C   Behavioral Flexibility with Analytics

BEHAVIORAL FLEXIBILITY WITH AMIABLES

Amiables

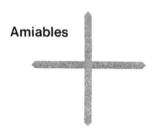

- Try to support the Amiable's feelings.

- Project that you are interested in your client as a person.

- Take time to effectively get the client to spell out personal objectives. Make sure you get the client to differentiate what he or she wants versus what he or she thinks you want to hear.

- When you disagree with the Amiable, do not debate facts and logic. Discuss personal opinions and feelings.

- If you and the Amiable quickly establish an objective and come to a fast decision, explore potential areas for future misunderstanding or dissatisfaction.

- Be agreeable with the Amiable by casually moving along in an informal, slow manner.

- Show the Amiable that you are "actively" listening and you are "open" in your discussions.

- The Amiable likes guarantees that actions will involve a minimum of risk. Offer personal assurances of support. However, do not overstate your guarantees, or you will lose your client's trust.

Figure 10-D   Behavioral Flexibility with Amiables

Behavioral Styles and Non-Manipulative Selling

The bottom line in non-manipulative selling is to establish trust and credibility with your clients. This requires an open, honest, and tension-free relationship. When you treat clients inappropriately, they feel uncomfortable with you, and their tension level rises. Trust and sales tend to decline.

Most of us accept that people are different and, therefore, need to be treated as such. The flexible salesperson can go one step further and identify these differences in people so as to treat them the way they want to be treated. The increase in trust, credibility, and sales opportunities make it worth the effort.

Part II

Non-Manipulative Selling: The Process

Communicating well with your client and building trust will take you a long way. Non-Manipulative Selling, however, will take you further yet. It provides a specific and unique way of applying the steps of the selling process. That is the message of Part II.

Chapters associated with Part II are:

11

Non-Manipulative Selling vs. Traditional Selling

MOST SALES transactions go through similar sales processes — information gathering, presentation, commitment, and follow-through. What goes on within those processes, however, spells a dramatic difference between traditional and non-manipulative selling approaches.

To better fit our purposes, we have renamed these processes as used in Non-Manipulative Selling as:

1. Define Need(s)/Problem(s).

2. Find a Solution.

3. Implement the Solution.

4. Track the Results.

Non-manipulative selling differs from the traditional sales approaches in two ways. First, non-manipulative selling stresses trust building and *centering on the client's real needs and problems* rather than using or creating needs to make a sale. Secondly, the amount of time generally spent at each of the four stages in the non-manipulative selling process is inversely proportional to that spent by the traditional salesperson. You can see this by referring to Figure 11-A. This is a direct outgrowth of what must be done within each process. The rest of the chapter provides an overview of the essential differences, and the following chapters detail each separate process.

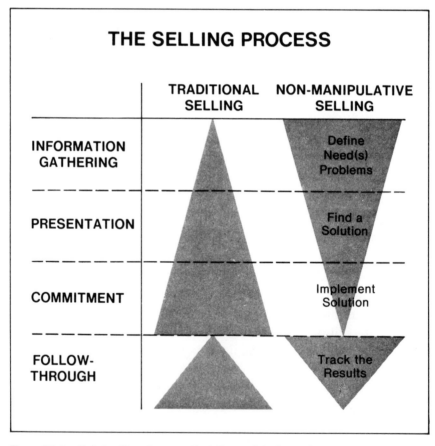

Figure 11-A   Relative Time Spent on Each Stage of the Selling Process in the Traditional and the Non-Manipulative Approaches

Information Gathering (Define Need(s)/Problem(s))

At the information gathering stage, the salesperson and client find out if there is something the client needs or wants for which the salesperson may supply help.

In non-manipulative selling, more time is spent on defining needs than on any other stage in the sales process. In any form of consultative selling, the client's problems or needs must be fully and accurately defined in order to effectively solve those problems or satisfy those needs. Then the rest of the processes evolve from a solid, accurate, informational base.

In traditional sales, this stage is limited. Much of the time is spent in "small talk" designed to break the ice. Little time is spent on defining the client's specific needs. In fact, the traditionally manipulative salesperson often *tells* clients their needs and moves quickly into the presentation process with an assumption that the client can't help but like product "X" when shown what it will do. Of course, many sales are made in this way; but the foundation is weak, and the client is the loser. When a non-manipulative salesperson with similar products and competitive prices comes along and spends time helping the client identify what is really necessary for doing business better, the client can become the winner. Chances are he'll recognize it and switch. Then who's the loser?

Presentation (Find a Solution)

Both traditional and non-manipulative selling methods allocate about equal amounts of time to the presentation process. That is where the similarity ends.

In non-manipulative selling, the presentation is both custom-tailored and participative. It is custom-tailored in that the salesperson only discusses the relevant aspects of the product or service as they relate to the specific needs or problems previously identified with the client's help. In addition, only a limited number of features are presented and they are presented in their priority of importance to the client. This allows the salesperson to spend more time on each of the high priority features of the product. As a result, client interest tends to be high and to be maintained. After all, it is the client's problem being tackled, not the salesperson's product being pushed onto a defensive buyer. Each non-manipulative presentation process is unique because individual client problems and their priorities are unique. There's no canned presentation here.

The non-manipulative presentation process is also participative. The client takes an active part in designing a new action plan to meet specific needs. The approach encourages the client to talk more and the salesperson to listen more.

The traditional manipulative salesperson enters the presentation process with little specific information on that client's needs. Even if the client has outlined his or her needs, the salesperson has no established method to assure that the client has stated them accurately; the traditional method focuses primarily on the product. Often the presentation is "canned" — memorized — to assure that the salesperson covers the crucial features. Frequently, a shotgun approach is used where each feature of the product is touched on while the salesperson looks for features that will interest the client. If the first few features are not relevant, the client tends to "tune out" the salesperson before the relevant aspects of the product or service are presented. But if the client doesn't listen, the presentation fails. Moreover, if the first few features are relevant, the time spent on them is no more than on the irrelevant features to follow. Another traditional approach is to focus on the assumed needs of the client. That's fine, if the guess is accurate; and some salespeople guess very well. If the guess is not accurate, the client's time is wasted. The non-manipulative selling approach eliminates the guessing.

Commitment (Implement the Solution)

The commitment process is the focal point in terms of time spent by the traditional salesperson. It is proportionately the least time-consuming for the non-manipulative salesperson. The traditional approach takes so long at this level because it involves overcoming objections and closing the sale. In fact, the raising of objections is really an information gathering situation placed late in the process. The importance of this approach was aptly discussed in an early sales book called *The Sale Begins When the Customer Says No!* The feeling at that time was that when a client said NO, then the salesperson was really able to exhibit his or her selling (persuasion?) ability — overcome the client's objections, and close, close, close! What effect do you think this approach has on the client's tension level — or the salesperson's?

The commitment process in non-manipulative selling is where the agreed-upon solution begins to be implemented. It does just the opposite as that of the traditional approach — it removes pressure; it occurs in an atmosphere of mutual trust and respect. No separation occurs between "selling" and "closing." With client problems, needs, and objectives mutually identified during the first stage of the sales process; with solutions arrived at mutually; with the client totally involved; the client commitment to the solution typically occurs at the end of the presentation discussions. The commitment process in non-manipulative selling, when deemed appropriate, becomes "when," not "if."

Follow-Through (Track the Results)

Another difference between non-manipulative selling and the traditional approach in terms of time and effort occurs in the follow-through process. The non-manipulative salesperson believes that the sale begins when the client says YES. At this point, the salesperson makes a commitment to the buyer to service and assist that client throughout their business relationship. The non-manipulative seller spends a lot of time at first establishing ways to be sure the service promised is the service provided.

Other sales techniques minimize this follow-through process. Of course, all salespeople keep in touch with customers, but so often the service concept is lost because of the stress on the product, not the client. And when a new sale is sought, the traditional salesperson has a lot to do that the non-manipulative salesperson needn't do because the service and rapport is already established.

Many salespeople are turning toward the idea of better follow-up. The non-manipulative selling approach gives ways to do it well.

After all, satisfied customers are a salesperson's greatest asset. They talk about the benefits they have derived from the product and the salesperson, and they often leave their listeners with a feeling that they, too, should buy from the same salesperson. Just as a satisfied customer becomes a source of future sales, a dissatisfied customer will prove to be a source of negative advertising and lost sales. Non-manipulative selling depends on long-term, trust bond relationships; and this is best accomplished through attentive after-sale service.

So, let's look at the processes in detail. Figure 11-A uses triangles to show you time-effort differences in the processes of traditional and non-manipulative selling. As we discussed the reasons for this time-effort difference, we suggested real and meaningful differences in the processes themselves. The next four chapters explore these more fully.

For those of you who find charts and figures helpful, we have provided flow diagrams to illustrate the central steps in the non-manipulative selling processes. They complete this chapter and will be referenced in the subsequent ones. Use them if you like. If you are not a fan of flow diagrams, you will be able to find the discussions meaningful anyway. These diagrams are only an aid, to be used or not used as you wish.

THE NON-MANIPULATIVE SELLING PROCESS*

1. **DEFINE THE NEED(S)/PROBLEM(S)**
   a. Establish the trust bond.
   b. Determine the current situation.
   c. Determine client goals and objectives.
   d. Identify client needs and problems.
   e. Agree on the needs and problems to be worked on.

2. **FIND A SOLUTION**
   a. Check the trust bond.
   b. Determine decision-making criteria.
   c. Solicit potential solutions.
   d. Suggest potential solutions.
   e. Agree upon the best solution(s).

3. **IMPLEMENT THE SOLUTION**
   a. Check the trust bond.
   b. Outline each other's tasks and responsibilities.
   c. Work out an implementation schedule.

4. **TRACK THE RESULTS**
   a. Check the trust bond.
   b. Identify criteria for successful results.
   c. Determine how and when to measure results.
   d. Monitor the results.

* All steps are to be done mutually with the client.

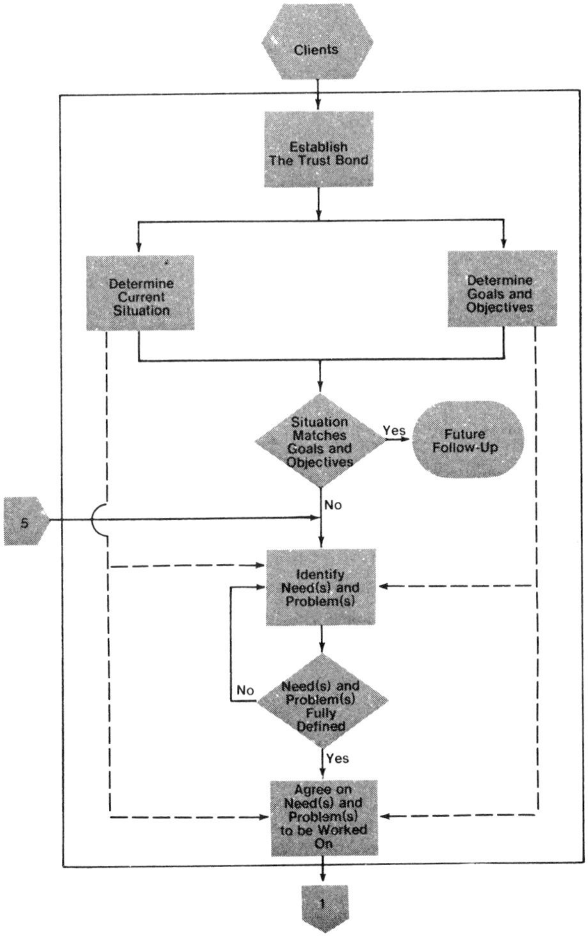

Figure 11-B   The Non-Manipulative Selling Process: Define the Need(s)/Problem(s)

THE NON-MANIPULATIVE SELLING PROCESS*

1. **DEFINE THE NEED(S)/PROBLEM(S)**
   a. Establish the trust bond.
   b. Determine the current situation.
   c. Determine client goals and objectives.
   d. Identify client needs and problems.
   e. Agree on the needs and problems to be worked on.

2. **FIND A SOLUTION**
   a. Check the trust bond.
   b. Determine decision-making criteria.
   c. Solicit potential solutions.
   d. Suggest potential solutions.
   e. Agree upon the best solution(s).

3. **IMPLEMENT THE SOLUTION**
   a. Check the trust bond.
   b. Outline each other's tasks and responsibilities.
   c. Work out an implementation schedule.

4. **TRACK THE RESULTS**
   a. Check the trust bond.
   b. Identify criteria for successful results.
   c. Determine how and when to measure results.
   d. Monitor the results.

* *All steps are to be done mutually with the client.*

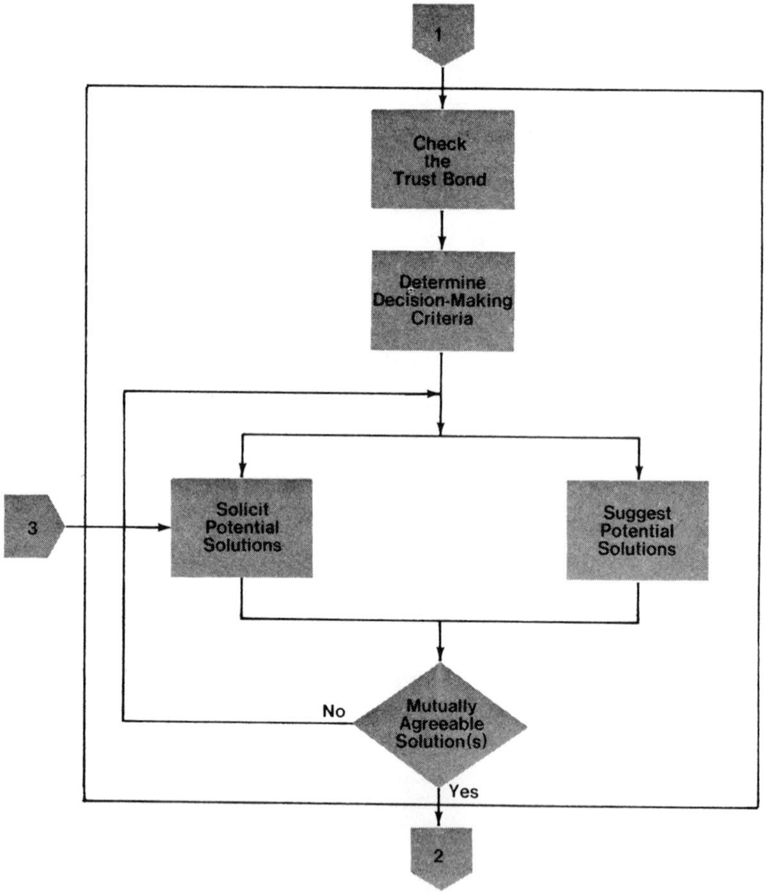

Figure 11-C   The Non-Manipulative Selling Process: Find A Solution

142

THE NON-MANIPULATIVE SELLING PROCESS*

1. **DEFINE THE NEED(S)/PROBLEM(S)**
   a. Establish the trust bond.
   b. Determine the current situation.
   c. Determine client goals and objectives.
   d. Identify client needs and problems.
   e. Agree on the needs and problems to be worked on.

2. **FIND A SOLUTION**
   a. Check the trust bond.
   b. Determine decision-making criteria.
   c. Solicit potential solutions.
   d. Suggest potential solutions.
   e. Agree upon the best solution(s).

3. **IMPLEMENT THE SOLUTION**
   a. Check the trust bond.
   b. Outline each other's tasks and responsibilities.
   c. Work out an implementation schedule.

4. **TRACK THE RESULTS**
   a. Check the trust bond.
   b. Identify criteria for successful results.
   c. Determine how and when to measure results.
   d. Monitor the results.

* *All steps are to be done mutually with the client.*

Figure 11-D   The Non-Manipulative Selling Process: Implement the Solution

143

THE NON-MANIPULATIVE SELLING PROCESS*

1. **DEFINE THE NEED(S)/PROBLEM(S)**
   - a. Establish the trust bond.
   - b. Determine the current situation.
   - c. Determine client goals and objectives.
   - d. Identify client needs and problems.
   - e. Agree on the needs and problems to be worked on.

2. **FIND A SOLUTION**
   - a. Check the trust bond.
   - b. Determine decision-making criteria.
   - c. Solicit potential solutions.
   - d. Suggest potential solutions.
   - e. Agree upon the best solution(s).

3. **IMPLEMENT THE SOLUTION**
   - a. Check the trust bond.
   - b. Outline each other's tasks and responsibilities.
   - c. Work out an implementation schedule.

4. **TRACK THE RESULTS**
   - a. Check the trust bond.
   - b. Identify criteria for successful results.
   - c. Determine how and when to measure results.
   - d. Monitor the results.

* All steps are to be done mutually with the client.

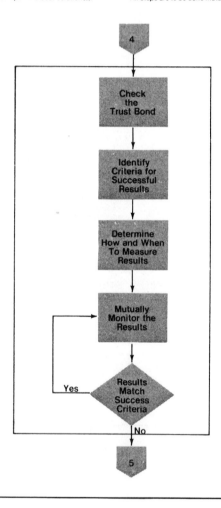

Figure 11-E   The Non-Manipulative Selling Process: Track the Results

144

12
The Information Gathering Process

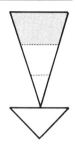

DO YOU want to make a sale — a good sale? The client wants to make a good buy. Both will be happier when the sale (the purchase) is built on a careful and systematic uncovering of the needs and problems which the product can meet and solve.

When you meet a client in a selling situation, follow the steps in Figure 12-A. Each step will bring you closer to helping the client identify particular needs and problems you can then help solve. As you go through these steps, you will be faced with opportunities to take different approaches based on your relationship with the client, the client's behavioral style, and the stage of the buying-decision process. What follows is a step-by-step approach to fulfilling the goals of Process 1: Define the Need(s)/Problem(s).

Step A: Establish an Atmosphere of Trust

High trust, low tension is the name of the game in non-manipulative selling. You begin to establish trust by the initial impression you create — if it is one of confidence and interest in the client. Think of the advice in the "Image" chapter, and think of

THE NON-MANIPULATIVE SELLING PROCESS*

1. **DEFINE THE NEED(S)/PROBLEM(S)**
   a. Establish the trust bond.
   b. Determine the current situation.
   c. Determine client goals and objectives.
   d. Identify client needs and problems.
   e. Agree on the needs and problems to be worked on.

2. **FIND A SOLUTION**
   a. Check the trust bond.
   b. Determine decision-making criteria.
   c. Solicit potential solutions.
   d. Suggest potential solutions.
   e. Agree upon the best solution(s).

3. **IMPLEMENT THE SOLUTION**
   a. Check the trust bond.
   b. Outline each other's tasks and responsibilities.
   c. Work out an implementation schedule.

4. **TRACK THE RESULTS**
   a. Check the trust bond.
   b. Identify criteria for successful results.
   c. Determine how and when to measure results.
   d. Monitor the results.

* All steps are to be done mutually with the client.

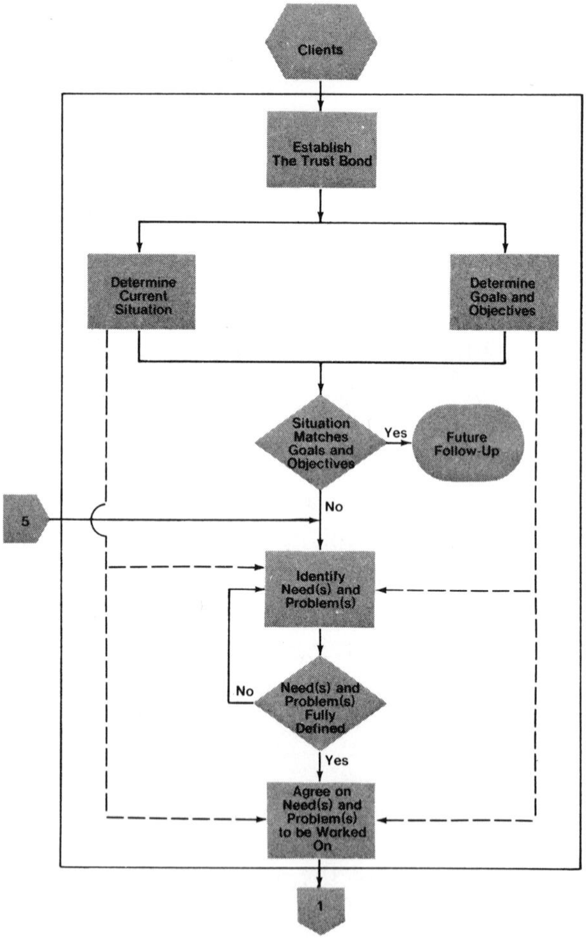

Figure 12-A   The Non-Manipulative Selling Process: Define the Need(s)/Problem(s)

146

situations where you feel you made an immediate positive impression. What image factors helped? Think of a situation that seemed to have problems from the moment you came into a client's area. What image factors could have hindered the start of a good relationship? And think, too, of the vocal qualities you projected and of your body language during this crucial initial stage.

Practice behavioral flexibility. In the initial stages of the sales interview and in establishing trust, how you interact with the behavioral style of the client may determine the positive or negative progression of the new relationship. If you are skillful here, you will definitely have an advantage. Remember, identify the style, confirm it, and modify your own style preferences where they are different from the preferences of your client. It really isn't all that hard to bite your tongue and refrain from telling the client about the latest news story if the client is an Analytic or Driver who wants to get down to business. Nor is it all that insufferable to hear about the Expressive's family vacation for a while before getting to the meat of the sales situation. Your sales relationship may depend upon it. Remember the importance of good initial probes to get your client to express thoughts and opinions and thereby allow you to more quickly determine the behavioral style preferences.

Apply your active listening skills, too. With these, your client feels immediately that you are listening because what is said is important. And it *is* important.

With careful and skilled use of behavioral flexibility and the communication skills, you not only establish trust but also build and maintain it throughout the sales relationship. Step A: Establish an Atmosphere of Trust, is a separate step, but it uses procedures and skills that should never be put away.

As you progress through the non-manipulative selling flow diagrams, you will notice that the first step of every process begins with your checking the level of trust before you move from a previous step into the major portion of the new process. To do this, remember that in establishing trust (or maintaining it), simply project to the client through your actions and words that you are sincerely interested in helping solve the client's specific problems and meeting that client's business needs.

Steps B and C: Determine the Current Situation; Determine Goals and Objectives

These two steps can be done in either order. Both pieces of information are important before you can begin to determine if a problem or need actually exists. For you to be of help, the current situation must not be meeting the goals and objectives identified.

Of course, both you and your client are interested in those aspects of the current situation that affect the product or service you can offer as a solution to a problem or need. So, focus your probing on these areas. (And remember to apply good probing techniques.) The same is true of your analysis of the goals and objectives; you need to focus on those pertinent to the problems and needs which your product or service can solve.

If you have done your homework and think you understand the current situation or the goals and objectives, that's great; but be careful. Listen to the client. Probe a little anyway. Check your findings. Otherwise, you could be like a salesperson who received a phone order from a foreign customer who needed trucks and, after being told the initial request of 100 was in error, only sent 10 (it was a poor country) by not hearing the subsequent request for 1,000.

The behavioral style of your client can provide a clue as to whether to determine the current situation or the goals and objectives first, all other things being equal. Suppose you are dealing with an Amiable style. Which of the two steps would you present first? Would you determine the current situation or identify the goals and objectives? The Amiable moves slowly and is comfortable in the present rather than racing toward the future. Moreover, the Amiable stresses relationships. Thus, a comfortable beginning with the Amiable is to first discuss the current situation. By slowly and informally exploring the current situation with the Amiable, you not only gather important problem-solving information, but you also sustain the budding trust relationship. This will help when you discuss the more task-oriented questions of goals and objectives.

How about the Driver? Which step is more appropriate to use first with this style of client? The Driver is extremely goal-oriented. The Driver will probably perceive you in a positive manner if you center on the goals and objectives. Generally, the Driver can provide them quickly and accurately. Then you can explore the current situation from the perspective of the goals and objectives. With this goal orientation, the Driver will work longer and more willingly than if you had begun with a general exploration of the current situation. After all, when you get to the current situation, you will be seen as helping explore ways to achieve those goals.

You are probably discovering that, even though non-manipulative selling has a step-by-step approach, the manner in which the steps are applied is determined by the style and needs of each individual client. Thus, non-manipulative selling is a unique and custom-tailored approach to developing long-term business relationships.

Remember that as you work with your client to identify and solve problems, your client will be listening to you for reasons to buy or not to buy from you. Many of the assurances will come out as the steps progress through the selling processes. The trust you establish and maintain will help. But be alert for chances to reassure the client in the following areas, provided that your assurances are honest — and only when:

1. The client needs your type of product or service.

2. Your product or service can actually satisfy the client's specific needs.

3. Your company will stand behind the product or service.

4. The price is fair.

5. You can provide the product or service as well or better than someone else.

Does all this sound complex? So would a description of riding a bike or driving a car. But people drive cars and ride bikes nearly every day without giving it a second thought because they have had time to absorb the processes. The non-manipulative selling processes are the same — they are simpler the more you use them.

Decision: Are the Goals and Objectives Met by the Current Situation?

Identifying the current situation, the goals, and the objectives may take many calls; or you may need only one. If you have done your job, you will have a picture of the actual conditions of the current situation and the desired conditions as revealed in the goals and objectives. Then compare them. How do they match?

When you have the two lists, you have a tool to help the client work beyond assumptions. Mismatches and no matches show up clearly. Sometimes, clients feel that the goals and objectives are being met when, in reality, they are not. Probing skills help here to identify with the client whether the goals are too narrow, not far-reaching enough (Amiables?), or too far-reaching (Expressives?).

Similarly, the current situation can sometimes be overstated or taken for granted. How often have you asked a potential client how their present plan of action was working, and they replied that it was working satisfactorily? Clients often believe this when, in reality, it could be better. A problem-solving, consultative salesperson is responsible for analyzing the current situation from all perspectives to make sure the situation is meeting the goals and objectives in the best way possible.

When the desired state (goals and objectives) and the actual state (situation) are fairly similar and working well, as shown in the left half of Figure 12-B, you can offer little or no improvement.

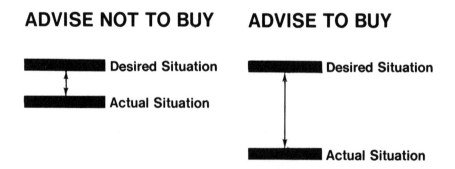

Figure 12-B   Distance Between the Actual and Desired Situation as It Affects the Buying Decision

End the sales interview. Going further may be fruitless and a waste of both your time and that of your client. You may be able to convince the client that your product or service is worth buying, but that would be satisfying your needs, not the client's needs. A true non-manipulative philosophy means that you cannot expect to sell everyone.

In the cases where you advise a client not to buy, place the client on a follow-up list. As time passes, the goals and objectives may change and the current situation may vary from them. Because of your initial no-buy advice, the client will most likely be eager to problem-solve with you again and trust your advice to buy, should that be the appropriate advice to give.

For instance, a washing machine vendor, upon looking at the goals of a laundromat owner, determined that the poor location (current situation) would sustain fewer machines than the owner wanted to order. Angry with the salesperson's advice, the owner went elsewhere and overbought from a salesperson glad to sell any number of machines — the more, the better. The initial advice was well founded; the location was so poor that it could not sustain the number of machines and the place closed. Since then, the person opened 14 new laundromats and has purchased all the machines from the vendor who had given the original advice not to overbuy. That's non-manipulative selling!

More often, the initial contact will reveal some way in which your product or service can be of genuine use to your client. The careful information gathering done by the non-manipulative salesperson helps both the buyer and seller identify this and trust it. (This situation is represented by the right half of Figure 12-B.) With a distance identified between the real and the desired situation, you are prepared to move on to the next step of Define the Need(s)/Problem(s). At this point, you actually specify what the needs or problems are.

Step D: Fully Determine the Need(s)/Problem(s)

This step requires a total definition of the needs to be met or problems to be solved. Only then can you and your client work together to generate a new situation which will meet the client's goals and objectives.

Look for root causes of the problems. If order forms are constantly misinterpreted, are the forms incomplete, the information poorly supplied, the vendor careless, the delivery system failing? Too often a cause is assumed; look for plausible alternatives before settling on the most probable cause(s). Another failing that results from quick assumptions of cause is that the symptom and not the real cause is attacked. It is like going to the doctor with a skin rash that you control with medication. The medication helps, but the real assistance comes when you identify that your plant in the living room is the culprit, and all you need do is remove the plant to stop the itch without medication. If a client needs better service, is it that more service calls are needed (that may help the symptom), or is it that a better communication of the problems when they occur needs to be established? Check the root cause.

Decision: Are the Problem(s)/Need(s) Fully Defined?

Checking to make sure the problem or need is fully defined is a safeguard against incorrect assumptions, against treating symptoms only, and against incomplete definitions. In other words, take some extra time and care to be certain you have all the information you need. Use your developmental and clarifying probing skills to ask the client to provide more information on problems or needs identified and to ask the client to confirm or correct what you already understand of the problems. You might give new information to the client in a probe aimed at stimulating additional thoughts on the issues at hand. Continue until you and the client are satisfied you have identified the cause of each problem under consideration.

Throughout all this, be aware of using all the communication skills you have to communicate interest, concern, and respect. Also, develop your communications with sensitivity to the pace and priority preferences of the client. Sustain the trust bond.

13

The Presentation Process

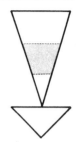

THE GOAL in finding a solution is to help your client find ways to improve the current situation. The stress is on (1) working *with* the client and (2) *improvements* over problems. Being *told* what to do is offensive to most people, and yet it is a real temptation, once problems are defined, to rush in with the answers. Resist and, instead, help your client as you problem solve together.

The model for Finding a Solution is shown in Figure 13-A. The ⓤ symbol is the beginning of the process and refers to the point at which you left the model in the last chapter.

Step A: Check the Trust Bond

The first step of this process is to check the trust bond. Remember that although maintaining trust is a continuing demand, pay special attention to the level of trust you have established before moving from one sales process to another. When the trust is high, moving on to another process is simple. When the

THE NON-MANIPULATIVE SELLING PROCESS*

1. **DEFINE THE NEED(S)/PROBLEM(S)**
   a. Establish the trust bond.
   b. Determine the current situation.
   c. Determine client goals and objectives.
   d. Identify client needs and problems.
   e. Agree on the needs and problems to be worked on.

2. **FIND A SOLUTION**
   a. Check the trust bond.
   b. Determine decision-making criteria.
   c. Solicit potential solutions.
   d. Suggest potential solutions.
   e. Agree upon the best solution(s).

3. **IMPLEMENT THE SOLUTION**
   a. Check the trust bond.
   b. Outline each other's tasks and responsibilities.
   c. Work out an implementation schedule.

4. **TRACK THE RESULTS**
   a. Check the trust bond.
   b. Identify criteria for successful results.
   c. Determine how and when to measure results.
   d. Monitor the results.

* *All steps are to be done mutually with the client.*

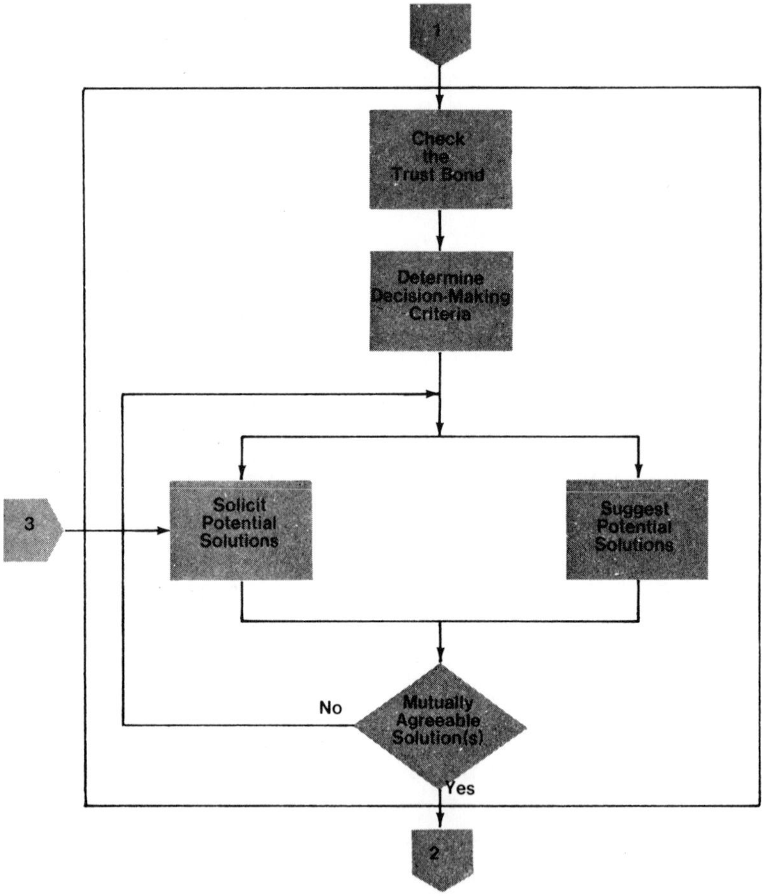

Figure 13-A The Non-Manipulative Selling Process: Find A Solution

156

trust is decreasing, the client is unprepared to make necessary decisions and is less willing to participate fully. The trust bond, like the marriage bond, needs constant work — or separation is likely.

Step B: Determine Decision-Making Criteria

Decision-making criteria serve to identify specific, measurable, attainable criteria which, when met, indicate the problem is solved or the need met. For example, the decision criteria may possibly be, "I need to reduce scrap material waste by 10 percent, avoid a reduction in product quality, and increase production by 5 percent at a minimum." If a client were that specific, wouldn't it be easier to help? If the figures were dream figures or unreasonable for some other reason, your help with making them more realistic is needed as much as your help in meeting realizable goals. The criteria result in solution objectives. One of the features of a solution objective, remember, is that the criteria can be attained.

Notice the characteristics of a good solution objective. First, it is *specific*. "I want to increase productivity by 5 percent," not just "I want to increase productivity." Second, the objective must be *measurable*. To say you want to increase employee morale is not as good a solution objective as saying that you want to increase employee morale and will recognize it by reduced sick leave days taken by 4 percent over the next three months (if appropriate). Third, the objectives must be *attainable*. We have sufficiently stressed this already.

A fourth characteristic is that the set of objectives must be *complementary*. To achieve one should not eliminate the achievement of any other. For example, if you wish to service your customers better, you might recognize this by a monthly contact of every customer and a weekly or biweekly contact for those who need more. But this may prevent you from meeting a goal of writing more lengthy and exacting reports (recognized by completion of established forms for each customer visited). Each goal is attainable in itself, but taken together, they are unlikely to be met. Strive for complementary goals which can all be met when considered together.

Steps C and D: Solicit and Suggest Potential Solutions

Armed with solution objectives, you and the client are ready to explore potential solutions. These are direct responses to the solution objectives and grow out of the information discovered during the initial information gathering phase.

Whether you or the client first suggest the solution, or whether you exchange ideas, what you do is take a look at the product or service in light of both the needs and the criteria by which the needs will be recognized as met. It is the matching of the benefits to the needs. Notice that you match benefits, not just features of your product or service. The features are basically the various parts that make it up. They are (physical) characteristics that exist regardless of who buys it or even whether it's bought or not. They answer the question "What is it?" On the other hand, a *benefit* is how an individual feature helps satisfy a specific need or problem on the part of the client. The benefit is the most important part of your product or service to know about. In reality, a client doesn't buy a product; he buys what it will do for him. The client buys the *benefits.* Products or services are means to goals, not ends in themselves. For example, the client does not view an advertisement as paper and ink alone. It is an investment for future gain or a means for self-esteem. Similarly, a movie theater is not just a building, projector, and screen. It is the means toward the benefits of relaxation, pleasure, and social interaction.

You raise the value of your product or service simply by allowing the client to discover the *benefits* received from owning it. Naturally, this means that you must be client-oriented. You must be sensitive to your client's needs. You should ask yourself, "Why would I purchase my product or service?" "How would it satisfy my needs?" "How would my product benefit me more than my competitors' products?" By having good, solid answers to these questions, and the honest belief that you and your product or service can truly benefit your client, you will be well on your way toward consummating more and more sales.

Your client's job in the suggestion process is twofold. As you suggest solutions, the client needs to respond and assist. Secondly, the client should suggest solutions. Many times, this is good to have the client do before you make suggestions. In this way, more of the solutions that eventually work may be the client's, not yours. Moreover, the client may come up with a fresh solution otherwise lost as you direct the effort down a different path.

You, as salesperson, have the job of presenting the features and benefits of the product or service which directly meet the needs identified and satisfy the solution objectives. Ideas that are short and set apart are easiest for your client to remember. This provides time to think about each one. Present your features and benefits one at a time and in their order of importance. The first feature/benefit should be the one that would have most personal or professional meaning to the client. Before discussing the next most important feature/benefit, get feedback to make sure the client understands how it can help. This is actually the process of "testing product acceptance." Have these feature/benefit feedback statements take the form of open questions. For example, "How do you feel this will help you meet your objectives?" "What importance does this have to you (or your company)?" or "What benefits do you think you might derive from this?" The feedback gives you some excellent clues about the readiness of your client to make a commitment.

View the presentation as a "discovery process" and not as a time for you to do all the talking. The whole idea of presenting features and benefits one at a time and getting feedback on each one before proceeding to the next fosters the two-way communication process. To ask your client how a specific feature can benefit him or her adds personal meaning to the presentation process and keeps your client involved in the buying process.

When you are satisfied that your client fully understands and accepts or rejects the importance of a given feature/benefit in solving a problem, you can then move on to the next feature/benefit, going through the same process. Present as many features and benefits as necessary to comfortably determine that your client is ready to make a commitment (to buy, not to buy, continue the search, etc.).

Of course, before you get into a sales situation you must prepare for it. As preparation, compare your product or service to your direct and indirect competition. What unique, positive features does your product have that competitive products do not have? What features does your product have that are of higher quality than those same features in your competitors' products? After compiling this strategic product (service) feature list, determine all of the benefits that each of these features provides for your clients. In completing this exercise, remember that often one feature can satisfy more than one client need. In other words, any one feature can have many associated benefits. In addition, any one client need can be satisfied with more than one feature. Keep in mind the critical importance of benefits. They build "value" on your product or service in the mind of the client.

Maintain the attitude that the solutions suggested are indeed "potential" and not "final." This avoids the pressure on the client and the problems associated with picking THE solution prematurely and then discovering that it doesn't fit.

This stage, like all the others in non-manipulative selling, is uniquely tailored to the specific needs of the client. It has to be, for the benefits you present and the order in which you present them are dependent upon the information you received earlier and worked on with your client. Each problem, each need, each client, the influence of time, and each set of priorities are different; so is each presentation.

Step E: Agree Upon the Best Solutions

When the solutions are analyzed and any solution is mutually acceptable to you and your client, it becomes, in effect, a psychological commitment on the part of the client. However, this commitment by the client is only one step toward the consummation of the sale. The implementation of the solution is the other crucial part; it is the physical part of the commitment. Until the client puts the new plan into action, do not count your commission. This is especially true of the Amiable style. Amiables may readily agree on a solution, but will have difficulty implementing it out of fear of trying something really new. Amiables are security conscious.

As a review, here are a few guidelines to remind you of some crucial communication skills.

1. Present solutions at a speed that is comfortable for your client so as to be neither confusing nor boring.

2. Whenever possible, use guarantees, warranties, testimonials, and the like, to reassure the client that what you are saying can be supported. This increases the believability of your presentation, especially with the Analytical style.

3. Get your client involved; let him respond to and suggest solutions.

4. Support your client for all contributive remarks.

5. Use voice intonation to emphasize important points, and pause for effect.

6. Avoid using technical industry language. Instead, speak your client's language.

7. If your interview is interrupted for any reason, briefly review the points last made before you continue with new information.

8. Constantly try to keep the presentation a two-way dialogue. Play the role of the sales "consultant."

9. Help your client visualize the benefits received from your product or service.

10. Use third-party testimonial stories with which your client can empathize and associate, especially with Expressives and Amiables.

When all solutions are acceptable to both you and your client, and when all solution objectives look like they have been matched with a solution — or reanalyzed and eliminated — you are ready to implement the solutions. Let's go on to the next chapter to see how it works.

14

The Commitment Process

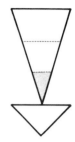

YOU MAY already notice that the separation between "selling" and "closing" is barely perceptible in non-manipulative selling. If the information gathering (Define Need(s)/Problem(s)) process and the presentation (Find Solution) process have been well done, the client has specified the needs and problems of concern and knows how your product or service will specifically meet them. You have had adequate chance to use verbal and non-verbal feedback to see how the client perceives your product or service as THE means to the goal. In fact, before you enter the implementation phase of the process, you and your client have mutually agreed on acceptable solutions to the problems identified. Therefore, the commitment is not "if" but "when!" Closing techniques are unnecessary, in the sense of radical, complicated, or manipulative techniques used to turn a sales situation around.

Step A: Check the Trust Bond

Figure 14-A provides the flow diagram for the implementation phase of the process. The symbol ② marks the entry point, the place where the last chapter (last process) left off. Once again, check the trust bond as your first step before actually moving into the new phase. If it is strong, go on to Step B. If it is weak, identify the source of the weakening links. Is it because something was not

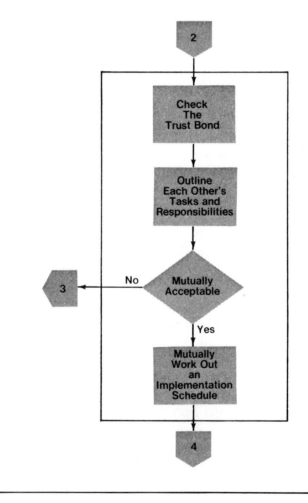

THE NON-MANIPULATIVE SELLING PROCESS*

1. **DEFINE THE NEED(S)/PROBLEM(S)**
   a. Establish the trust bond.
   b. Determine the current situation.
   c. Determine client goals and objectives.
   d. Identify client needs and problems.
   e. Agree on the needs and problems to be worked on.

2. **FIND A SOLUTION**
   a. Check the trust bond.
   b. Determine decision-making criteria.
   c. Solicit potential solutions.
   d. Suggest potential solutions.
   e. Agree upon the best solution(s).

3. **IMPLEMENT THE SOLUTION**
   a. Check the trust bond.
   b. Outline each other's tasks and responsibilities.
   c. Work out an implementation schedule.

4. **TRACK THE RESULTS**
   a. Check the trust bond.
   b. Identify criteria for successful results.
   c. Determine how and when to measure results.
   d. Monitor the results.

* *All steps are to be done mutually with the client.*

Figure 14-A   The Non-Manipulative Selling Process: Implement the Solution

fully cleared up? Is it because you began to respond less to the style preferences of the client and more to your own preferences? What can you discover? Of course, the check is a rapid one, made as you are completing the last phase. A possible way is to have Analytics and Drivers summarize previous decisions or considerations. Provide a break for Amiables and Expressives or have them state the possible effects of the decisions or considerations on their personal job satisfaction. While you are listening to their responses, listen also for the way they respond and indications of involvement — or lack of it. And if the bond is weak? Tune up all your communication and flexibility skills, check for thorough understanding of the processes on the client's part, and only then move on to Step B.

Step B: Mutually Outline Tasks and Responsibilities

Verbally clarify and confirm what each of you — the salesperson and the client — will do to make the solution work. Follow this with a written agreement concerning who is to do what, by when, and how. (This is besides the contract associated with the sale of a product or service.) To avoid misunderstandings and loss of trust, be sure to specify and solidify the details of the mutually accepted agreement. It is the salesperson's responsibility to do this — not the client's. This avoids those embarrassments and greater damage done to a sales relationship when the client receives a COD shipment instead of an expected 90-day credit. Even if the mistake is explained away and the sale doesn't cancel, the salesperson in this situation loses credibility and competence in the eyes of the buyer.

This outlining of tasks and responsibilities is important with all styles, but be especially careful as you do it for Amiables and Expressives. Both styles are more prone toward relationships than tasks, and unless the tasks are put into writing with appropriate deadlines, the tasks may (unintentionally) not get done. The Expressive with a characteristic lack of concern with details and tasks may actually forget anything from making an appointment for an insurance physical to providing crucial figures for a formula that would make your job easier for you and cheaper for him. Provide the structure that Expressives can't seem to, or don't want to, provide for themselves.

With Amiables, be careful that you do not too quickly establish an objective that may very well result in later hesitancy or change. Outline the tasks, when you do arrive at a decision, in realistic and concrete terms. Be very careful only to state what you can or are willing to do, or you will, by promising too much and not coming through, destroy your trust bond rapidly with an Amiable. In addition, explore together potential areas for misunderstandings or dissatisfaction. An Amiable who is unhappy or dissatisfied will not readily talk about the feelings in an effort to avoid conflict. You may not have an inkling of your client's feelings until after business is given to a competitor with whom the client feels more comfortable and trusting. Therefore, when you explore areas of dissatisfaction and misunderstanding as you outline tasks and responsibilities, you will know beforehand when to recognize potentially detrimental situations. Keep your own notes on this.

As you outline the tasks and responsibilities, any time a conflict or problem arises in what you both understand, handle it then and there. Often, you will be able to negotiate mutually acceptable terms or redefine the tasks and responsibilities. At other times, the tasks or responsibilities, as understood by one of you, remain unacceptable. If so, return to the beginning of the second process, Find a Solution. It will take extra time, but it is worth it. A potentially damaging problem has been uncovered early when it can be handled and defused.

Step C: When Do We Proceed? (Implementation Schedule)

With a mutually acceptable solution and a list of tasks and responsibilities mutually drawn up, you and your client are ready to proceed to the last step of the implementation process. To do this, ask the client an open question that requests direction, such as "Where do we go from here?" or "When do we proceed?" Because of all the previous preparation, this question is an open, straightforward request, lacking the pushy, tricky, and manipulative characteristics of other closing or assumptive questions under other situations. Since your client has participated fully in the entire sales transaction and has had a major hand in arriving at the solution, you will generally be answered with a time, date, or other relevant reference. If there is something for concern, your client will generally by this time feel comfortable and trusting enough to speak out. You are, after all, problem solvers working together. There is no "Objection Game" when the mutual trust level is high.

So far, this is all very simple. You ask an open question or an assumptive question and the prospect positively commits. What happens, however, if the prospect does not commit at this point? In the past, salespeople have typically reacted in an aggressive manner. Get the objection, overcome the objection, ask for the order — and on, and on, and on. This does not seem right. This method raises defenses, increases tension, and reduces trust. Instead, handle the problem. Objections usually come from one of four specific reasons:

1. You haven't collected enough information.

2. You have been working with wrong information.

3. The trust bond hasn't been fully developed.

4. You have misjudged your client's behavioral style and are treating him incorrectly.

5. There are technical problems over which you have no control.

If the reason for no commitment is incorrect or insufficient information, you need to determine where and why you went wrong. Did you gather the wrong information, give erroneous or incomplete information, or was there simply a breakdown in the feedback process? In any of these cases, you have to go back to the point of communication breakdown, start all over, and use this new information to design a new plan that may better suit the needs of your client.

Objections stemming from wrong or insufficient information can usually be corrected simply by providing new information. The three-step process to use in dealing with "easy" objections is:

1. Clarify the objection, if necessary.

2. Answer the objection directly.

3. Confirm your answer.

For instance, a client may say that your service is desired only if you can implement it immediately. You may want to clarify what "immediately" is before you go any further. Depending on this clarification, you may be able to meet immediate requirements. In that case, you *directly answer* the concern. Finally, you *confirm* your response to make sure that it fully and satisfactorily answered the concern.

Other objections which lead to an unsold client are more difficult to handle. Some of them occur when the trust bond is broken or if you mistakenly identify behavioral style. If trust is lacking, try to use your communication and trust-building skills to reestablish that bond (if it is not already too late). If you misjudged your client's style, you probably have been interacting inappropriately. Start treating the client according to the client's style needs. It may reestablish your rapport and salvage the sale.

Even with high trust sales situations, technical problems may be beyond your control and result in a lost sale. For instance, the client may want an inventory for a transfer of ownership and insist that the inventory be taken on a date which is already sold out. Or you may be expected to provide a color or style of item that is no longer available. Unless the date, color, or styles can be changed, the sales cannot be consummated; they are beyond your control. These problems are the difficult ones. When appropriate, use the following three-step process in dealing with difficult objections:

1. Clarification

2. Compensation method

3. Confirmation

In this approach, Steps 1 and 3 are similar to Steps 1 and 3 for easy objections. The difference lies in Step 2. The compensation method acknowledges deficiency in a particular area, but tries to "compensate" for it by using other unique or quality features to outweigh the shortcomings. If you can't meet the date, suggest other times and stress the advantages of the sale. If you don't have a requested style or color, present options you do have and identify benefits of using the product you sell. This method is especially effective when the service or product shortcoming is not one that has a very high priority to the client, for alternatives often appear attractive.

During the implementation phase of non-manipulative selling, you will have your most difficult time with Amiables and Analytics. The Amiable style is slow-moving, risk-avoiding, and security-conscious. Amiables like guarantees that the actions to be implemented involve a minimum of risk. Offer the Amiable client your *personal* assurances that you will stand behind the actions agreed upon. This step will often take gentle, slow, but firmly directive action on your part to give the Amiable the confidence to follow through. If you handle your encouragement and prodding in a personal manner, the Amiable will generally go along with the plan. Remember, this prodding is not the prodding of an unwilling client, but the encouragement of one who has gone through the entire process as a partner in problem-solving.

The Analytic style is also to move slowly and avoid risks. This style also has a strong need to be right. Analytics are not as slow in implementing decisions as are Amiables IF they are SURE their actions cannot backfire. Provide the Analytic personality with the tangible, factual guarantees that provide the needed assurance.

Drivers and Expressives generally provide neither resistance nor hesitation at this point. They usually want to get on with it now that they have come this far.

After the client has committed to a specific time to proceed, both client and salesperson are ready to enter the final phase of the non-manipulative selling model — Tracking the Results.

15

The Follow-Through Process

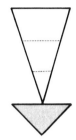

FINALLY, THE commitment — the last major step, the "extra mile" you go for your clients is here. It is the follow-through you make to build future sales. But it is not the follow-through represented in a phone call or by keeping in touch so that new products can be ordered. That occurs also, but this follow-through is more, and it involves some initial extra effort on your part that the traditional salesperson doesn't have to expend. But then, it has its payoffs. Professional salespeople realize that they can maintain and expand their sales volume simply through servicing and cultivating their current customers.

First, to prevent problems, put yourself in your client's position. The old adage, "Don't criticize a man until you have walked a mile in his shoes," certainly goes for customer service. This approach gives you great feeling for client problems; and the better you can get into your client's "shoes," the better you can work together to solve future problems and meet additional or changing needs.

Second, develop an attitude of sincere friendship, respect, and concern. The more you give of these, the more you will receive from your clients. The working relationship that grows from this is a strong one that resists destruction. Clients who return these feelings will be extremely hesitant in changing to another product or service.

Third, provide your client with thoughtful service. Here are some suggestions:

1. Maintain frequent contact, if only by phone or letter. The longer and more profitable the client's relationship, the more frequent should be the contacts.

2. Always have a good reason for contacting clients. Dropping in on them is thoughtless, for they have schedules and demands on their time too and appreciate being able to plan for you.

3. Check to see that your client has what he should have when he should have it.

4. Periodically, inquire about the client's experience with the purchase. Determine if help is required in any area in which you or your company can be of service.

5. Determine how the customer is currently using the product or service and suggest alternative uses, where appropriate. Many times, clients are unaware of the full range of tasks or services a product can supply.

6. Where possible, reasonable, and appropriate, supply your client with materials to aid in doing a better job.

7. Inform your clients about trends, new products or service requirements, and any other developments which may be of interest to them.

A well-serviced client repays you in recommendations, testimonials. support, and sales. Plan your customer service and other follow-through activities carefully. You will be respected — and expected. On this basis, you enter a long profitable business relationship with your client. Both sides win!

Step A: Check the Level of Trust

Enter the last section of the non-manipulative selling model at point ④ of Figure 15-A. Again, check the trust bond and work at enhancing it. As a matter of fact, not only are the trust-building communication and flexibility skills practiced as you follow-through, the entire follow-through process helps you to maintain and enhance the trust bond with your client. Most salespeople fail to follow-through in the helpful spirit of the non-manipulative selling approach, and this activity itself will set you apart.

Step B: Identify Criteria for Successful Results

After you are comfortable with the level of trust (or are consciously working at improving it), work with the client to identify the criteria that will determine whether the results achieved by the product or service purchased were successful. These criteria are best considered with the client's overall goals and objectives in mind, and they usually are the same as the solution objectives of the "Find a Solution" process. Be certain to focus your identification efforts on the time and quantity elements of the solution objectives. Is your client seeking a 10 percent return on investment, a 25 percent decrease in employee absenteeism, a 6 percent increase in sales? Are the goals specific, measurable, attainable, and complementary? Further, when does your client expect to achieve the results identified — in two months, six months, one year? These specifics give you and your client firm benchmarks by which to measure and compare actual results.

Step C: Determine How and When to Measure Results

Once the criteria is firmly set, you can determine with your client what and how to measure to see how well the criteria is met. Without common agreement, both you and your client may measure the criteria differently and lose a common ground for discussion, improvement, and agreement. Then whose figures indicate the success? If your figures are positive and your client's are

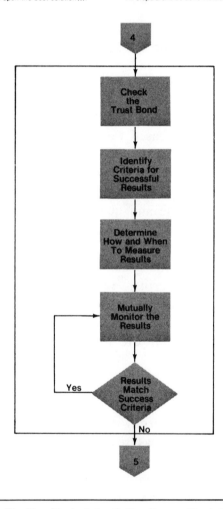

THE NON-MANIPULATIVE SELLING PROCESS*

1. **DEFINE THE NEED(S)/PROBLEM(S)**
   a. Establish the trust bond.
   b. Determine the current situation.
   c. Determine client goals and objectives.
   d. Identify client needs and problems.
   e. Agree on the needs and problems to be worked on.

2. **FIND A SOLUTION**
   a. Check the trust bond.
   b. Determine decision-making criteria.
   c. Solicit potential solutions.
   d. Suggest potential solutions.
   e. Agree upon the best solution(s).

3. **IMPLEMENT THE SOLUTION**
   a. Check the trust bond.
   b. Outline each other's tasks and responsibilities.
   c. Work out an implementation schedule.

4. **TRACK THE RESULTS**
   a. Check the trust bond.
   b. Identify criteria for successful results.
   c. Determine how and when to measure results.
   d. Monitor the results.

* *All steps are to be done mutually with the client.*

Figure 15-A   The Non-Manipulative Selling Process: Track the Results

negative, how do you take corrective action, if you do at all? If your client's figures are positive and yours are negative, you would be right in taking corrective action; but will your client agree to a possibly disruptive activity? Will you have the courage — the guts — to admit your product is weak when your client's figures show a stronger product? If you never set down figures, will you even try to communicate with your client as to the measured results? Get your figures established and avoid all this conflict.

For example, when I sell a client a sales training program for a sales force, the client generally expects certain results from the training. These results are typically spelled out in the solution objectives which we derive. A typical client objective is to increase the sales of each attendee. Now, let's add the detail: Say that the increase of sales for each attendee is to rise 5 percent. OK? If I stopped here, I might assume the client wants that result within a year. My client, however, wants it to happen within six months. Can you imagine what might result from this misunderstanding? It might be especially bad if the client's goals are truly reasonable only at the longer time span. Had we adequately communicated, we could have discussed the potential problem.

With clearly specified quantity and time dimensions, we can now determine how and when to measure the actual new performance to see if it is successful or not. As several ways to do this are generally available, it is once again important to decide the specific procedures with the client. For example, we can measure sales by:

1. Sales volume in dollars.

2. Sales volume in units sold.

3. Sales volume by type of customer.

4. Sales volume by type of product or service.

5. Sales volume versus dollar quota.

6. Sales volume versus unit quota.

7. Sales volume versus last year's sales volume.

8. Sales volume per sale.

9. Average sales volume per sales call.

10. Percentage of actual sales to sales calls.

11. Amount of new customer sales.

12. Average sales volume of seminar attendees versus average sales volume of the rest of the sales force.

If you think that the previous measures of sales productivity might provide some decision problems, take a look at additional measures of sales performance that can be used to determine a salesperson's performance:

1. Number of new accounts sold.

2. Number of current accounts lost.

3. Gross profit of a salesperson's territory.

4. Net profit of a salesperson's territory.

5. Sales expenses in relation to sales volume.

6. Number of customer complaints.

7. Number of customer praises.

8. Number of prospects contacted daily.

9. Average order size.

10. Percentage of cancellations.

So, with all these available methods, which do you select? You choose, but do so WITH your client. To fail to do so will invariably cause problems — I speak from experience.

Most of the forms of measurement, so far, are numerical. However, sometimes you may wish to use subjective measures. For instance, might you not think that people who go through my seminar should say they thoroughly enjoyed it? A postseminar questionnaire will allow them to express their attitudes. Likewise, isn't it essential that the salespeople retain the seminar material? You can measure this too. Therefore, when you and your client identify criteria for successful results and plan forms of measurement, remember some of these more "subjective" dimensions of successful results.

Now, when do you implement the measures? This, too, needs to be decided mutually to avoid problems. Be sure to specify both when and how often. Especially get this down if your client is an Expressive. Otherwise, that client will overlook the details and fail to do his part of the measurement process. Analytics, on the other hand, may create other problems by overdoing the measurement (either by measuring too often or too much). Therefore, get it down in writing. Confirm the process, and all will go well (or at least more of the process will be smoothed out).

Step D: Monitor the Results

Finally, run the results and compare the results with the criteria established. If the new performance meets the criteria, take no other action than to continue to monitor and measure the new results at specified times, as planned. If, on the other hand, the new results do not measure up, determine the problem(s). To do this, return to the "Define the Problem" process at point ⑤ , shown in both Figures 15-B and 12-A. At that stage, you initially matched the client's current situation with the desired goals and objectives. Notice the similarity with the comparison of the new performance (the actual) with the success criteria (the desired). Back in "Define the Problem," if the current situation matched the goals and objectives, you scheduled the client for regular future follow-up. In "Track Results," if the new performance matched the success criteria, you simply followed the scheduled follow-through process. But then in "Define the Problem," if the client's current situation did not match the desired goals and objectives, you went on to determine the problem(s) which caused the divergence. Likewise, in "Track Results," if the new performance fails to match the success criteria, determine the problem causing the divergence. Sound familiar? It is. That is why, when the new performance does not meet criteria, you re-enter the process at point ⑤ of the "Define the Problem" section. The non-manipulative selling system is, therefore, a closed-loop system. With a new solution and new criteria, you establish new measures and dimensions and again run the measurement and test it against the criteria. If they match, continue to monitor and measure; if they fail to match, proceed to point ⑤ of "Define the Problem."

Interestingly, second and subsequent times through the entire process with the same client usually are not as time-consuming as the first effort, given a firm trust bond and the previous experience at arriving at the needed decisions.

"Track Results" is the last step of the last process in the non-manipulative selling process; and yet, at the same time, it is the first step of an ongoing system of selling that you can successfully use with each and every client for the rest of your sales career. It assures that you do those things which encourage strong trust bond relationships and future sales.

16

Where Do You Go from Here?

IMAGINE WHAT would happen — to you — if you successfully applied the principles and practices of non-manipulative selling. Other people who have used non-manipulative selling claim increases in sales. Many state that they experienced a remolding of themselves into a professional and respected consultant. Still others point out an increased ability to contact and sell to major decision makers. Others have found it easier to work with fellow employees. What do you want as your goal? Where do you go from here?

One thing you can do right away is set some goals for yourself and establish a plan to meet those goals. To do this, apply the following three steps:

1. Accept the challenge.

2. Make plans to develop your non-manipulative selling techniques.

3. Apply non-manipulative selling techniques on the job.

Accept the Challenge

Non-Manipulative Selling works, and its skills can be learned. Of course, all the skills take practice, and you won't fall into them without work. But the processes and skills have proven rewards.

Even beginners in the approach can experience some of the benefits. So accept the challenge and also accept that, although you won't become expert overnight, the very fact that you want to uncover needs and problem solve with your customer will take you a long way in the right direction.

Make Plans to Develop Your Non-Manipulative Selling Techniques

So you've accepted the challenge. Now you need to meet it. With so much to learn about identifying behavioral styles, about using communication techniques, and about applying the steps of the sales processes, where do you start? How do you create an effective plan that meets your needs?

My advice is that you first apply some of the non-manipulative selling process steps to your own situation. For instance, what is *your* current sales situation? How well do you currently identify behavioral styles? How well do you probe? — listen? — use body language? — give feedback? How flexible are you in responding to different behavioral styles? As you determine your current situation, identify where you want to do better and how you will recognize when you are doing better. For instance, I might decide I want to be able to identify behavioral styles. I will be happy when the style I initially ascribe to 80 percent of the people I meet seems to be their actual style, as verified over repeated visits. That's my goal. Remember, though, the customer who is goal setting has the advantage of a professional guide (the salesperson) who makes sure the goals are realistic. If you set your own goals, they may be too difficult — or too easy. With this caution, go ahead and list these goals. Compare them with your current situation, and prioritize them according to your needs. Then create a plan.

Your plan might include further professional help in the form of seminars, books, or tapes. It can also involve practicing skills with a friend or two or, as implied in the "Listening" chapter, some of the skills can be practiced alone.

Your practice will probably include a more detailed review of relevant portions of this book. Other practice might involve asking a friend to role play with you. Still other practice might be to start identifying the behavioral style of familiar people so that you begin to have benchmarks against which to compare and rate strangers.

Whatever your goals, do make a plan. Otherwise, you may get caught in the morass of trying to do too much at one time and not really growing acceptably with any specific skill.

Recall that making a plan is followed in the selling process by tracking the results. Planning how you will recognize realistic growth in each area of concern is a rewarding activity. I suggest — no, encourage — it heartily.

Apply Non-Manipulative Selling Techniques on the Job

Of course, your practice allows you to apply the skills of non-manipulative selling on the job. And you needn't wait; you can start to apply the skills immediately. If your listening skills are not well tuned, for example, attempt to use them anyway. This is far better than ignoring an important technique as something you'll think about some other time. The same goes for identification of behavioral styles and applying behavioral flexibility. You can use these skills right away, even before you are very good at them. You may, however, wish to *concentrate* on one skill at a time, adding to your repertoire as you progress.

To apply the non-manipulative selling processes requires some special preparation. You will need to add a review of the processes to your usual precall homework. That will help keep you from stepping as frequently into old habits of hurried problem analysis, canned speeches, and the "Objections Game."

Correctly used, non-manipulative selling allows for information gathering in an open, honest atmosphere of trust and helpfulness. The client gains solutions to identified problems. The salesperson gains the support of a client who is fully committed to solving the identified problem. The non-manipulative salesperson deservedly feels pride in a rewarding sales profession.

The path has been shown. Where do *you* go from here?